Ex Libris

CHRIST CENTERED MINISTRIES
P. O. Box 824
Denver, Colorado 80201

DAVID FORBES MORGAN, O.C.C.M.

CHANT

The Origins, Form,
Practice,
and
Healing Power
of
Gregorian Chant

KATHARINE
LE MÉE

BELL TOWER NEW YORK

Published by Bell Tower, an imprint of Harmony Books,
a division of Crown Publishers, Inc., 201 East 50th Street, New York, New York 10022.
Member of the Crown Publishing Group.

Random House, Inc. New York, Toronto, London, Sydney, Auckland

Bell Tower and colophon are trademarks of Crown Publishers, Inc.

Manufactured in the United States of America
Design by Linda Kocur
Endpapers from a liturgical manuscript written and used in a Spanish convent
during the first half of the sixteenth century

Library of Congress Cataloging-in-Publication is available upon request.

ISBN 0-517-70037-9
10 9 8 7 6 5 4 3 2 1
First Edition

CONTENTS

CHAPTER 1

WELCOME TO CHANT

There is a smile spread across the whole world. Born of love and the spirit of gentleness, it has made its way into the hearts of millions of people of all ages and all walks of life. The smile is carried on a glorious song, the sound of Gregorian Chant, sung by the Benedictine monks of the small Spanish monastery of Santo Domingo de Silos, located high on the Castilian plain, near Burgos, in north central Spain. From a remote monastery, which served for hundreds of years as a rest stop for pilgrims on their way to worship at Santiago de Compostela, has come music that refreshes and restores by its deeply spiritual nature and by the generous and gracious way it is sung.

The recording of the singing monks, known in the United States as *Chant,* was first released in Spain as a double-disk album in the fall of 1993. Highly acclaimed throughout Western Europe, it was introduced in America in March 1994, this time as a single compact disk and an audio cassette. To the astonishment of everyone—producers, the listening public, and the monks themselves—the recording soared not only to number one on *Billboard's* classical chart but to number three on its pop chart as well. Attaining a rating of Gold in three weeks and Platinum in five, *Chant* kept on singing its way around the world until, today, almost 4,000,000 recordings have been sold and the album is available in more than forty-two countries.

Quick to add its fire to the general enthusiasm, the press took up and embellished the story of the black-robed Benedictines and their phenomenal success: their singing was "Preparation for the Millennium," "Monk Rock," "Nothing short of en-chanting," "A Hit 1,000 Years in the Making." Glorious sounds, pure and simple, sung in a language most could not understand, widely attracted the attention of even the younger generation, who flocked to record stores to pick up their copy.

The recording, made on several occasions during the last twenty years at the Monastery of Santo Domingo de Silos, has nineteen offerings, all taken either from the context of the Roman Catholic Mass or from the daily devotional services sung by the monks. The Latin chants follow closely upon each other, allowing only the space of a breath, so that the listener's attention is held close throughout the recording. Some of the music is seasonal: *Puer natus est nobis, et filius datus est nobis: cuius imperium super humerum eius,* "A child is born to us, a son is given to us: his shoulders shall bear princely power." Some harks back to the ancient Hebrew scriptures: *Os iusti meditabitur sapientiam, et lingua eius loquetur iudicium. Lex dei eius in corde ipsius,* "The mouth of the just one shall meditate wisdom, and his tongue shall speak judgment. The law of God is in his heart."

We also rejoice in hearing the song of a pilgrim approaching the gates of the holy city: *Lætatus sum in his quæ dicta sunt mihi: in domum domini ibimus.* "I rejoiced when they said to me: 'We will go unto the house of the Lord.'

The words of the *Improperium* spoken by Christ at his moment of greatest need, "My heart has expected reproach and misery: I looked for someone to grieve with me, but there was none, and to comfort me, and found no one," speak poignantly to us today when we, also, suffer loneliness and rejection.

If we are open to receiving the music, and it appears that the number of people who are increases daily, it comes to us easily and with no sense of strain. We have only to listen carefully to its gentle rise and fall. The sound is effortless, the result of conscious practice. It makes no unwanted intrusion, yet is ready to welcome us whenever we wish for its warmth and clarity. It beckons us to sit down and rest, to enjoy not only the lovely melodies but also the silence from which they come and to which they regularly return.

The chants are always sung in perfect unison, each note clear and even, any harmony that would distract us conspicuous by its absence. In the chant there are no climactic moments that we might eagerly await and from which we would return, exhausted of our emotional substance. Instead, the musical line is constantly nurturing, feeding our inner emotional life without exciting superficial feelings. If we are unfamiliar with the text, it is difficult for us to know exactly how we should be reacting. Perhaps the message is that we should simply not react at all, but be content to rest in the serene and wakeful presence that the music evokes.

Because of its intimate connection with sacred words of scripture and with devotional practice, Gregorian Chant has the power to awaken the mind and heart, of both singer and listener, to deeper levels of being. This is music that has been given heightened consciousness by the careful and attentive practice accorded it by monks and nuns throughout the centuries. The spirituality and authenticity that we perceive in the recording derives in no small part from the way that the monks live and the attitude of devotion and love of God with which they sing.

Medieval people were well aware of the formative power of music. They knew that setting lines of scripture to song would imprint them ever more deeply into the memories of the worshippers, and that the words' effect would be sustained over longer periods of time, with greater intensity. They also knew that sound is causal, that it can bring about changes in the very nature and fabric of society as well as within the individual.

It is therefore not surprising to observe in our own day that music has been potent enough to rock and roll its way behind a seemingly impenetrable Iron Curtain. In the same way that the long blast of the ram's horn, the sound of the trumpets, and the great shout of the people were enough to flatten the walls of the ancient city of Jericho, it would seem that popular music, hammering at the minds and hearts of people for less than a generation, did perhaps more than standing armies and diplomats to bring down the Berlin Wall.

As these shock waves of sound have been battering Eastern Europe, they have also been pounding on our societies in the West, and results are everywhere apparent: a loosening of the social structure, ever more disorder in the streets and within families. It is impossible to listen to anything over a period of time without being affected by what we hear.

Perhaps the current enthusiasm for Gregorian Chant indicates that we, as a society, are beginning to prefer quieter, more subtle sounds. Maybe it is unnecessary, now that the bricks are down, to crush them into dust. We could just as well pick them up and do something useful with them. In the cacophony of pneumatic hammers, there may be room for a few concrete mixers and molding forms!

A friend, native of Cameroon and currently in political exile in the United States, tells of spending four years in prison in his native country twenty years ago. The prison governor, himself a member of a tribe different from that of most of the prisoners, imposed a daily regimen of two hours of singing Gregorian Chant. The ostensible purpose was to occupy the prisoners and prevent them—at least during the time of singing—from plotting any further insurrection in a language unfamiliar to the governor. The chant, however, had an additional and more far-reaching effect, of which the governor was probably unaware, and that was to preserve the sanity and nourish the minds and hearts of the prisoners. Here was a constructive use of music.

Music is so abundantly available and so close at hand for most people in our society that we have come to take it for granted. We expect it while the dentist is preparing to drill or while the jet is getting ready for takeoff. Imagine having to keep up aerobic exercises for an hour without some energetic music to prod us along! The recent introduction of classical music, piped into New York City's Port Authority Bus Terminal, makes waiting there tolerable and provides a sense of cheerfulness and order. Everywhere we turn there is music of one sort or another, used for purposes limited only by our creative imagination. We turn it on and off almost without thinking, sometimes oblivious, for better or worse, of the effect that it is having on us.

Chant is very much with us today, not just as a beautiful recording of liturgical music from Spain, but as something in which we ourselves can participate. More and more people are engaging in the practice of "sounding" or "toning," which means singing prolonged sounds, usually simple vowels, on a single note. All faith traditions have available sounds that hold and embody their sacred teachings and that have the power to bring about greater devotion and heightened states of consciousness. A great deal more attention is now being accorded to the practice of these sounds, both for their devotional content and for their healing power.

Like medieval people standing at the brink of the end of the first millennium, we find ourselves wondering what the end of the second and start of the third will hold in store. It is clear, and can perhaps be seen in the tremendous response to the recording of *Chant*, that we as a people are seeking wisdom and spirituality. There is a need not just for new ideas, for something more to look at and consider from the outside, as it were, but for something that we can actually experience.

In order to appreciate fully what chant can offer us, we need to spend a little time becoming used to a mind-set quite different from our own. In medieval art, architecture, and worship there was nothing that was purely arbitrary. The artist, composer, or worshipper followed patterns or rituals that were determined by tradition and the sacred art of number. One has only to study closely the floor plan of a Gothic cathedral to see that its seeming complexity and originality result from the repetition of a single symbolic pattern.

In medieval numerology the number seven stood for the completed event, the coming together of forces divine and earthly. The octave, with its seven intervals (*do, re, mi, fa, sol, la, si, do*), was a perfect illustration of the way in which all events were structured. If we sing or play this scale, we can gain a little idea of how this progression was viewed: *Do* is the beginning, the strong initial idea that determines the whole ascent. *Re* is a note that marks the first tentative steps toward realization of the idea. Here it is easy to be dissuaded, and the note may lose its resolve and return to the *do.* The quality of *mi* is pleasant. The first step has been taken and we know that the climb is possible, maybe even enjoyable.

At this point in the octave comes a step unlike the two previous ones, from *do* to *re* and from *re* to *mi.* Although the step is perceived as smaller, real effort is needed here in order to continue. If one thinks of the way that the word *Amen* is often rendered musically (*fa* back to *mi*), one can appreciate the fact that the *fa,* somewhat poignant in quality, may still return whence it came, that is, down to *mi,* and eventually back to *do* . . . or it may climb higher.

The quality of the *sol* is completely different. This is a bright, triumphant note. Whatever was uncertain before has been resolved. Energy and enthusiasm are abundant, helping us to press on. *Sol*, referred to as the dominant note of the octave, is tremendously full of power.

The octave continues to the note *la*, a note that loses some of the brilliance that was so apparent in the *sol*. Here the upward direction is unmistakable but there is also a quality of resignation, "Thy will be done on earth as it is in heaven."

At *si* there is absolutely no turning back. The top *do* beckons and the *si*, recognizing total inability to resolve the octave through its own doing, accepts the mercy and grace offered from above and comes into full union with the top *do*, which is twice the number of vibrations per second as the opening *do*. The octave is then complete. Whatever was envisaged at its inception has come into perfection.

The octave was seen by medieval people not only as governing the development of the music but as determining the proper sequence of all other significant events. Everything was made to conform with laws that were viewed as inherent in the very nature of the world.

We can talk and think about the fascinating numerology so omnipresent in the medieval world view, and this is very useful for our understanding. However, there is something further that escapes our grasp, and that is the mysterious sense of presence evoked by the conscious art and liturgy of the Middle Ages. As revealed in the chanting of the monks, there is a quality that defies explanation.

Our modern attempts to understand everything, dramatically illustrated, for better or worse, by the use of the vernacular language in today's Mass, may have the effect of cutting our religious experience off before its full flowering. It has always been true that what is "up front" is only part of the story. For the initiated—and perhaps sound is our gate of entrance—there is always something more to be experienced. Jesus reminded his followers of this when he said, "Those who have ears, let them hear."

You are invited now to enter the medieval world where the historical and liturgical sources of Gregorian Chant are to be found. There will be an opportunity to spend time in the monastic setting—long enough to hear what the monks might say if they were allowed to speak to us. Without actually finding a room at Santo Domingo de Silos we can, in our imagination, follow the monks as they sing the sacred music of the church, throughout the day and the year.

The single most important point to retain is that Gregorian Chant is liturgical music, designed to embody the holy words of Christian scripture. It is filled to overflowing with spirit, which can be heard in the singing of the monks. We can be grateful to them for sharing it with us.

CHAPTER 2

MUSIC AND THE MEDIEVAL WORLD VIEW

The medieval period, or Middle Ages, during which Gregorian Chant developed, spans a period of more than 800 years, from the 600s to the 1400s. It has often been considered a dull and dark moment, a hiatus between the Greco-Roman glory and the enlightenment that began with the fifteenth-century Renaissance.

However, there was no clear break at either end of the period; instead there was an evolution from a Roman empire to a Frankish one, under the umbrella of the rising spiritual and temporal power of the papacy. Compared to the brilliance of Rome, there was, at first, a setback in civilization. But slowly a recovery began and bore its first fruits in the Carolingian renaissance at the turn of the ninth century. In 789 Charlemagne ordered schools to be opened in each diocese and each monastery for the benefit not only of the clergy but also of lay children. He invited to his court men of talent from other countries—Italy, Spain, and particularly England. The most famous among them was Alcuin, a monk and a man of letters from York, who became, also, a missionary and apostle of Latin Christian culture in France. He is celebrated to this day as its preceptor. With the death of Charlemagne, the new empire was partitioned, and this first revival of learning soon lapsed into indifference, except in a few centers. With the approach of the millennium, a mood of gloom and despair again overtook the land.

When the year 1000 came and failed to bring about the anticipated catastrophe of the end of the world, a great relief was felt throughout Christendom. Hope was rekindled, and the energy released by this expansion of spirit transformed Western Europe, leading eventually to the twelfth-century renaissance. This was the high point of the Middle Ages. It provided new directions, and its resonances are still very much with us today.

The twelfth century impressed a new form on our intellectual life with the founding of the universities; it saw the rise of national consciousness, the formation of new social classes, and the growth of vernacular languages and literature; it gave birth to new modes of argumentation in law, and to fundamental developments in logic and grammar. Art, architecture, and engineering flourished. The Church developed a potent organization and systematized theological thought. All told, the twelfth century exhibited a cosmopolitanism and an interest in wider horizons not unlike that of our own times.

The medieval period was therefore anything but homogeneous. The state of society moved from the chaos of the fall of the Roman Empire to the high point of the twelfth century and then fell back again, in the fourteenth and fifteenth centuries, into another chaotic period marked by the Black Death, the Hundred Years' War, and feudal anarchy.

This evolving and disparate world was held together, however, by a central force, Christendom, formed by all Christians throughout the world, collaborating toward the religious purpose of the Church; it was the domain of Christ and the potentiality of his second coming. As the light of the Roman Empire dimmed in the fifth and sixth centuries, its congregations and monasteries preserved and nurtured whatever shreds of learning and civilization escaped the onslaught of the barbarians. Besides the scriptures and the writings of the Church Fathers, among whom Augustine occupied a prominent place, those of Boethius and Dionysius, in particular, had a seminal influence in forming the medieval world view.

Boethius

◆

Boethius (480–525) was born at the moment when the Western Roman Empire had ceased to exist as an entity. He was a high official in the imperial administration, which the new Visigoth masters were trying to oversee. A Roman, a Christian, and a man of culture, he was familiar with Plato and Aristotle in the original Greek and with the later developments of Neoplatonism. He is now primarily known for his *Consolation of*

Philosophy, which he wrote while in prison awaiting his execution, having been charged with treason for causes that are still unclear.

Early in life Boethius decided to translate into Latin and write a commentary on the complete works of Plato and Aristotle. He had only just begun this monumental work when his life was brought to an abrupt end, but he did leave behind translations of the work of Euclid, Ptolemy, and others on geometry, arithmetic, and music. He also wrote textbooks and treatises on these subjects and on theology and education. Medieval schools were greatly indebted to him, not only in terms of subject matter but also of method. Boethius was the first to apply Aristotelian logic to theological problems and the elucidation of dogmatic statements on which scholasticism was to be founded. He is therefore the direct ancestor of the scholastic method. His contribution was unique and many-faceted. Music theory, which not only is at the basis of Gregorian Chant but also forms the very foundation of the medieval world view and infuses its thinking, was learned from him.

Dionysius

◆

Another body of writings that were mystical rather than philosophical and scholastic, produced around the same period, had an even greater and more durable influence than those of Boethius. These writings, known as the *Corpus Areopagiticum,* comprise five works—*Mystical Theology, Celestial Hierarchies, Ecclesiastical Hierarchies, Divine Names,* and *Ten Letters.* Their author called himself Dionysius, a disciple of Paul. Early on he was identified as Dionysius the Areopagite, who had been converted upon hearing Saint Paul preach in Athens. However, modern scholarship has established that these works were produced in the fifth century, contemporary with Boethius, and were probably written by more than one author, perhaps of Syrian origin. To indicate their apocryphal character, their author (or authors) is often referred to as "Pseudo-Dionysius," or "Dionysius the Mystic."

In the days when authorship was not considered as exclusive as it is today and when a writer was more intent on the dissemination of his work than of his name, it was not unusual for someone to pretend that his work had been written by an authority in a previous century. The effect was to ensure these writings a respect that they might not otherwise have received.

Although it is only eight pages long, *Mystical Theology* remains one of the most imposing mystical constructs in the history of Christian thought. As the contemporary French scholar Georges Duby writes,

> At the core of the treatise was one idea: God is light. . . . The universe, born of an irradiance, was a downward-spilling burst of luminosity, and the light emanating from the primal Being established every created being in its immutable place. But it united all beings, linking them with love, flooding the entire world, establishing order and coherence within it.

Mystical Theology inspired the development of Gothic art, architecture, and engineering in the twelfth century. The principles of this short text permeate the music of the entire period, giving it its radiant quality.

Music as a Model of the Universe

◆

In medieval times music theory informed not only musical composition and performance, but proportion in architecture and structure in society. It was also understood to regulate the health of the body and explain the very workings of the universe. All of these things depended on harmony, the *tranquillitas ordinis* of Augustine. The thinkers of the Middle Ages accepted Boethius's legacy and with it the musical thinking of the Greeks from Pythagoras and Plato on.

The curriculum, first in the monastic schools, then in the cathedral schools, and finally in the universities, was based on Boethius's teaching. First came the study of language and mathematics—a very modern program indeed, but also a very ancient one, since naming and counting are two primordial activities shrouded in our mythological beginnings, practices that make us human. The medieval curriculum consisted of the trivium (grammar, rhetoric, and dialectic) and the quadrivium (arithmetic, geometry, music, and astronomy). The function of these subjects was to prepare the mind and heart for the study of philosophy and theology. The Gospel of John starts with the words "In the beginning was the Word," and so language was considered the foundation of everything. Even the Old Testament states that the first act of Adam was to name things. But equally important was number. For Saint Augustine, "construction of the physical and moral worlds alike is based on numbers."

To medieval thinkers, arithmetic, the science of number, was fundamental. Music was the expression of number in time, giving pitch, duration, rhythm, stress, and accent to the words. Language regulated by number was the song. Number structuring space was geometry. Number in time and space gave rise to the cosmic dance or the harmony of the spheres: astronomy. Even philosophy and theology were under the sway of numbers: Three was the mysterious Trinity and seven the divine number—a whole sacred arithmetic applied to the theological universe. But if number was the abstract principle underlying the laws of the cosmos, music was its manifestation in creation. Like the

Pythagoreans before them, the Fathers of the Church and the Schoolmen perceived the universe as essentially musical.

Musica mundana (the music of the world or the spheres), *musica humana* (the music of man), and *musica instrumentalis* (instrumental music, including the human voice) were the three kinds of music governing creation. Everything obeyed the same mathematical laws: the astronomical and theological, the political and moral, the medical and musical. Music was the very essence of the nature of things, and to sing was to align one's body with the laws of nature and one's mind and soul with the laws of God.

Music theory in the Middle Ages was, therefore, vastly more comprehensive in scope than it is today. It was more akin to modern physics but, of course, it was much more inclusive, since it ranged from the physical to the psychological and spiritual. It acted as an integrating factor, bringing together the different value systems of the culture. In contrast, our present culture gives us a sense of disintegration. Different areas of knowledge are parceled out to various departments; mathematicians have little to say to theologians, physicians to astronomers, and even physicists of various specialties do not quite speak the same language. More sadly, perhaps, all do not seem to be overly concerned with the preoccupations of our common humanity. Medieval society had a clear, common purpose: the salvation of souls and the establishment of God's kingdom on earth. This required the combined energy of those who pray, those who fight, and those who work—clergy, knights, and laborers.

Following the Pythagoreans, and the Neoplatonic ideas filtered through Boethius, music was perceived as creating unity within multiplicity, the union of opposites, accord within discord. An important element in music was the octave, a succession of eight notes having five large and two smaller intervals. As the music theorists could show, due to the arithmetical inequalities of certain tones, intervals could not be piled upon one another without compromising the octave. To extend the range of creativity beyond the octave, one was reduced to working with modes or something had to be given up: either the integrity of the octave or the purity of the interval. The best solution was to keep within the octave or close to it. To go beyond was moving into another world, another range of being. Thus chant melodies tend to stay within the range of a single octave.

The problem met by the ancient musicians who discovered that trying to be consistent in the octave led to inconsistency in the intervals is somewhat parallel to difficulties we have with our mathematical and physical theories. In 1931 Kurt Gödel, a German mathematician, came up with a so-called Incompleteness Theorem, which shows that there are truths that cannot be demonstrated formally, even in so simple a system as arithmetic. In other words, a formal proof of consistency, that is, of complete coherence, generates an inconsistency in the system. Another modern parallel is that of the Uncertainty Principle, defined about the same time by Werner Heisenberg, a German physicist, whereby the more we know about one aspect of reality (such as the position of a particle) the less we can know about a related aspect of that reality (such as the velocity of the same particle) or, extending this to a linguistic example, the more we specify the usage of a word, the less meaning we can get from it.

These principles seem to be telling us something the musicians of the Middle Ages knew experientially—namely that, fundamentally, there always remains a place, a gap, that escapes our control. In this there is grace, for it brings to the human heart a degree of humility and curbs the arrogance that too easily fills it when it thinks it knows everything.

The relationship in musical models between the particularity of notes and the wave aspect of sound is reminiscent of the particle/wave complementarity of modern physics. This may account, in part, for the remarkable ability of musical models to provide a satisfactory guide to human understanding. It has often been remarked that modern physical theories such as quantum mechanics bear certain analogies to musical theory. This may simply reflect the musical background and biases of the builders of these theories, but it also points to the common ground between ancient and medieval thought models.

The thinkers of the Middle Ages had discovered in the Greek heritage a rich musical tradition that can also be traced back to the Babylonian, Sumerian, Egyptian, and Vedic cultures. Musical models are able to enshrine the knowledge of the universe in a very compact form, and a song or hymn built on harmonic principles embodies this knowledge. It is not simply "information," a mere abstraction of reality, but a participatory, active knowledge reflecting the inner nature of things and revealing itself only through the performance of the song. As played on the instrument of the heart, mind, and body of the performer, the song's knowledge becomes a living reality. In this way the singers become a medium between heaven and earth, the worlds of cause and manifestation, bringing their listeners into direct contact with higher worlds. In that moment, living in accord with the laws of heaven and earth, they resolve the dissonances within themselves and within their audience, spreading healing through their song.

The ritual becomes sacrifice, and the singing, an act of worship. Hence the anonymity so puzzling to our individualistic perspective. For today we want maximum freedom *for* ourselves, while the traditional artist looked for freedom *from* himself. For the medieval artist, all actions originated in God and returned to God. That is why on the portal of the church of Pont-Hubert near Troyes in France the anonymous medieval master mason wrote,

Non nobis Domine, non nobis,
Sed nomine tuo da gloriam.

Not unto us, Lord, not unto us,
But to your name let glory be given.

It is interesting to contrast the medieval approach to understanding the world and our present-day mathematical approach. The models used by all traditional civilizations and particularly by the medievals were musical and therefore had a mathematical basis, but they addressed the sense of hearing. By contrast, modern models are purely mathematical. They are abstract. When data or results have to be translated for interpretation, the medium is visual, which remains an intellectual, surface experience. The sense of hearing, however, connects experientially with the heart, and music and sound touch us most directly. We do not resonate so deeply with the visual as with the auditory. This may be explained by the fact that our visual apparatus has a frequency range of slightly less than one octave, from infrared to ultraviolet, whereas our auditory system has a range of about eight octaves, approximately 60 to 16,000 hertz, or number of vibrations per second. We are sensitive to sound frequency as pitch and to light frequency as color. The frequencies of the visual field are much higher than those of the auditory field (by an order of 10^{10}) and, as is well known, the higher the frequencies, the lesser the penetration of a given material. For instance, a piece of cardboard shields us easily from the light, but it takes a thick wall to block out sound, and the lower the pitch the deeper the penetration. We are very sensitive to sound, not just through the ear but through our whole skin, and all our organs are affected by it.

No matter what artifice is used, visual display remains essentially a two-dimensional experience, governed by the laws of perspective. Hearing, however, is by nature three-dimensional, an experiential means of generating space. It follows that the experience in the case of the visual and mathematical model remains that of an external observer, detached from the object of observation, whereas that of the listener is participatory, with the listener right in the middle, not detached and observing from some remote viewpoint.

More important, perhaps, music brings together two fundamental aspects of number, the quantitative and the qualitative. The quantitative involves the number of notes per beat when there is one and the volume of the sound, while the qualitative is concerned with the appreciation of the value of an octave or an interval or the effect of the tone on the hearer or singer. Numbers and their musical representations are, in this perspective, states of being. *One*, for instance, is not just a figure on a page or a digit in a computation or an item on a shelf, but unity, unison. As Theon of Smyrna put it, "Unity is the principle of all things and the most dominant of all that is: all things emanate from it and it emanates from nothing."

As an experiential model, music disciplines the mind, gives it a norm of reference with the octave, and imbues it with the significance of hierarchy. Abstract mathematical models miss many of these qualities. Here, again, what we gain in precision we lose in meaning.

The Octave and Esoteric Tradition

◆

An esoteric tradition has come down to us concerning the octave. It has been linked with wisdom schools through the ages, from the Egyptians, the Greek mysteries, and various Roman philosophical schools down to such institutions as the Florentine Academy of Marsilio Ficino and Lorenzo de' Medici in the fifteenth century. There is no doubt that this knowledge, alluded to in Chapter I, was available within certain influential circles in the Church during the Middle Ages, as the architecture of its buildings abundantly shows.

According to this approach, the octave, sometimes called the Law of Seven, is really the law that governs the time succession of events, while each event is itself the result of three forces. Boris Mouravieff, in his study on the esoteric tradition of Oriental Orthodoxy, explains that between *mi* and *fa*, and *si* and *do*, corresponding to the semitones of the musical scale, special attention must be paid so that the octave proceeds normally. Otherwise the progression may be deviated or slowed down, even stopped altogether. P. D. Ouspensky makes the same point in *In Search of the Miraculous* and gives the example familiar to everyone of working through a project where,

> after a certain period of energetic activity, work becomes tedious and tiring, moments of fatigue and indifference enter into feeling; instead of right thinking a search for compromises begins; suppression, evasion of difficult problems. But the line continues to develop though now not in the same direction as in the beginning. . . . If, however, at the necessary moment, that is at the moment when the given octave passes through "an interval," there enters into it an "additional shock" which corresponds in force and character, it will develop further without hindrance along the original direction.

This concept of the Law of Octaves can be traced in most of the developments of traditional civilizations, from the architectural arrangement of temples and the organization of ceremonies, to the composition of literary works. In Chapter 4 we shall see how the Mass, one of the daily ceremonies in which the monks participated, is arranged according to this scheme.

Music and Wholeness

◆

For Thomas Aquinas, beauty had three requisites: perfection, harmony, and clarity. So does wholeness. These are qualities of the soul. They are of God, but they reflect and are reflected in music, in the body, in society, and in the cosmos.

Music was viewed as having the power to order and unite the whole of creation. In society then, as Plato said, "The companions of right reason are decency, cadence, and accord; decency in song, accord in harmony, cadence in rhythm." The function of music was not to impose humanity's desires on nature but, through reason, to open human receptivity to the natural order.

Gregorian Chant is a conscious musical form designed to ennoble singer and listener through its intrinsic beauty, its wholeness, and the immediacy of its performance. It has sustained monastic communities for 1,500 years; it helped bring together the empire of Charlemagne; it impressed a definite character on the Roman Church; it played an essential role in the evolution of Western music. Its ancient melodies still have the power to inspire, transform, and make whole.

The world view of the Middle Ages may appear to us limited and quaint, a closed spherical system with earth standing still in the middle while planets, sun, and stars move in concentric circles around it to the tune of unhearable harmonies. Of course, we know better now. We have walked on the moon and sent probes to the limits of our solar system. We have discovered galaxies and black holes and we understand that our planet is but a speck in a remote recess of the universe. We even view the solar system as chaotic. But we may be reading the score too closely. In the process we seem to have forgotten the music. Once, it had the power to restore order and harmony to the whole and wholeness to the parts. Perhaps listening to chant will rekindle in us the vision of William of Auvergne (1180–1249), who said, "When you consider the order and magnificence of the Universe, . . . you will find it to be like a most beautiful canticle . . . and the wondrous variety of its creatures to be a symphony of joy and harmony."

CHAPTER 3

A HISTORY OF EARLY
WESTERN CHANT

Jewish Roots and Early Christianity

◆

The beginnings of Western chant are found in traditional Jewish worship. The early Christians were, themselves, Jews who chose to follow the teachings of Christ, finding in his life, death, and resurrection their own way to salvation. There is very little information available to us, from our vantage point nearly two thousand years later, about how the early Christians actually carried out their worship or the specific music that they used. One thing is sure: the powers that be in Rome took a very dim view of what the Christians were doing, forcing them to adopt clandestine practices such as meeting in the city's subterranean catacombs, a series of tunnels normally reserved for the burial of the dead. One can imagine that small groups of people would also gather together in homes, behind closed doors, keeping their songs quiet and brief so as to attract as little attention as possible from the Roman authorities.

Scholars have succeeded in matching some of the oldest Western chants with early Jewish melodies. It would have been natural for the early Christians to continue to sing already familiar songs, perhaps changing the words over a period of time to reflect their new experience and beliefs. Since the earliest sources indicate that the music was sometimes sung with the soloist and congregation alternating, it was more than likely that a cantor from the synagogue, someone with a personal inclination toward the new religion, would have been invited to participate and lead the singing.

For the newly forming Christian community the evening was the preferred time for worship, the moment of quiet balance as day turns to night, when candles are lit to illuminate the darkness. The Jewish tradition of beginning the Sabbath and every day in the evening was strong in the memories of early Christians. It was also preferable to organize secret meetings during the night rather than to risk being discovered in the bright light of day.

Music was generally learned by heart through repetition. Most probably the earliest chants were a heightened mode of speech, where each syllable of the text was sung on a single tone of comfortable pitch. The notes would have been sung in a balanced, steady manner with perhaps introductory notes and a change of pitch up or down either at or near the end of the line. This example in English illustrates the method:

The Spi - rit of the Lord fills the whole earth

It might even have been common to sing two or more notes to some syllables, dividing the time evenly between them. Try chanting this example for yourself:

The Spi- rit of the Lord fills the whole earth

There is no reason to believe that this early music was in any sense rigid. There were probably a number of Jewish folk melodies, perhaps even accompanied by simple instruments, that made their way into the worship, causing mixed reactions, as happens with such practices even today. It is well known that, by the second century, some of the early Church Fathers found instruments too distracting and folk melodies too heretical in their content to be allowed in communal worship. From the third century on, for about five hundred years, only the unaccompanied human voice was considered appropriate. This is still the practice today in the Russian Orthodox Church, although in the West instrumental music gradually found its way back into the liturgy. By the tenth century bellows organs were found in cathedrals and monasteries, and by the thirteenth and fourteenth centuries the portative organ, pumped and played by the same person and capable only of monophonic music, was extensively used. Apart from the organ, the only other instruments generally allowed in church were small bells, or cymbala, suspended in a row above the player and struck with a hammer. Their use, like that of the organ, was strictly regulated by liturgical custom.

Much of the early chanting was done in a direct style, in which a soloist or a group sings the song from start to finish. Since the purpose was to cause the words and the feelings they engendered to affect not just the mind but also the body and the heart by penetrating them deeply, the lines were often repeated and there were a number of different ways of singing them. Sometimes soloist and congregation would alternate; sometimes the congregation was divided to sing alternate verses and then came together for a refrain. These ways of singing have remained a part of Western chant through the centuries to the present.

The early Christians continued the singing of Psalms and reciting of prayers that had long been part of Jewish traditional worship. Soon added was the agape, which was a meal eaten together in a spirit of love. For the participants this meal, consisting of bread and wine and taken at the traditional evening hour, was the fulfilling of the commandment given by Christ to his disciples on the night of the Last Supper, "Do this in remembrance of me." It thus became a commemoration of the life and sacrificial death of Christ, taking on the form of a mystical ritual where the elements of bread and wine were viewed as truly transformed into the body and blood of Christ. As time went on the Greek word *Eukharistia,* "thanksgiving," was adopted. This Eucharist has remained the central act of Christian worship ever since.

During the first two centuries of the Common Era there is ample evidence that the hours for worship were increased to include not only the sunset or Vesper hour but also a service in the night (Vigils or Matins), and another at daybreak (Lauds). The practice of remembering God at frequent intervals during the day was soon fully developed in the context of monastic life.

The Eucharist or Mass (taken from the Latin expression used at the conclusion of worship, *Ite missa est,* "Go, you are dismissed," when worshippers are sent forth to carry Christ's message into the world) became a more formal service. It included many of the elements that are still used today: prayers, readings from the Old and New Testament (which are now the Christian Bible), a sermon, the offering of the bread and wine, the greeting and exchange of the kiss of peace, and the Eucharist itself. Certain prayers or texts were constant and frequently used, while others changed to fit the day or season of the Christian year; this practice would eventually yield the Ordinary or fixed sections of the Mass, and the Proper or changeable parts.

The third century saw the further development of what was still an oral musical tradition. Hymns, many of which were based on popular melodies and folk tunes, came to be used. They provided a good opportunity for congregational participation and were a joyous addition to the services. Athanasius, patriarch of the church in Alexandria in the fourth century, is quoted as saying that the Psalms should be sung with such moderate inflection that they sound like speech rather than singing. Yet by his time there began to arise a body of chants of considerable sophistication.

The Use of the Latin Language
◆

A few words are necessary here about the language in which the words were sung. In Palestine the liturgy of the early church continued to be celebrated in Aramaic, the language spoken by Jesus. However, when the Apostles began to carry Jesus' teachings farther away, they adopted Greek, which was the international language of the time, much as English is today. A very flexible language, Greek was well adapted not only for recounting stories of the life of Jesus, but also for supplying a rich technical vocabulary for the organizational and doctrinal formulations of the early church. The apostle Mark wrote for the Roman community in Greek and Paul the Apostle also composed his Epistles to the Romans in this language.

The idiom used was not the Greek of classical antiquity but rather the *koiné* or vernacular language of small traders, travelers, colonists, and others who had been driven from their homes east of the Roman Empire by war or economic need and had established themselves in the big cities and ports of the west. It was among such humble people that Christianity found its first converts. The Kingdom of Heaven was promised to the poor and had tremendous appeal to these simple folk.

Gradually there must have been an increase in the number of Latin-speaking converts among what was at first a community of Greek and bilingual Christians. The early Christians evolved a language that was a combination of both Greek and Latin, an idiom largely incomprehensible to those outside the faith. It would have been replete with terms from both Greek and Latin, as early scriptural texts attest. Many of the Greek technical terms denoting ideas foreign to the pagan world would of course have had no equivalents in Latin. They were therefore simply transliterated and became part of the language of Latin Christianity. This fact explains the presence of words and expressions such as *apostolus,* "apostle"; *angelus* "angel"; *baptisma* "baptism"; *ecclesia* "church"; and *Kyrie Eleison,* "Lord have mercy" that occur in the chants.

A language reflecting the speech habits of the early converts to whom the Gospel was preached, Latin slowly gained precedence over a period of time. It gained new dignity as the vulgar (that is, common, of the people) language was used more and more in the context of worship. Eventually its use in the scriptures and liturgy was to have a profound effect on the most highly educated and cultivated Roman Christians. The most sophisticated of writers made no effort to reform or correct what was essentially an idiom of the people. Even Saint Jerome, responsible for translating a Greek version of the Bible into Latin at the end of the fourth century, left many of the "vulgarisms" of the older texts untouched. His translation, referred to as the Vulgate, came to be used, in revised form, as the Roman Catholic authorized version.

No doubt the creation of the vernacular Latin language used in the earliest chants took place over a long period of time and involved people of widely diverse backgrounds. The result was an ecclesiastical language ecumenical in character and widely accepted by the Christian community over an extremely large geographical area stretching from Italy westward to France, Spain, and southern England, and southward to the entire coast of North Africa. The apparent consistency of the language was due in no small part to the constant coming and going of missionaries and other church representatives, who saw the spreading of the good news of Christianity as their primary purpose in life.

The End of the Persecution of the Christians

◆

During the first three centuries after the birth of Christ persecution of Christians was particularly severe, especially under the rule of the Roman emperor Diocletian (reigned 284–305). However, all this changed when Constantine, emperor from 306 to 337, himself came to espouse the new religion. During a battle with Maxentius, his rival for imperial power, Constantine saw in the sky a blazing cross bearing the motto *In hoc signo vinces*, "By this sign thou shalt conquer." Thenceforth he had the cross placed on his banner, and his troops went into battle with Christ's name on their shields. Constantine eventually defeated Maxentius in 312, and in 313 he issued the famous Edict of Milan, which granted all Christians freedom of worship and recognized the Church as an institution having the right to own property. Later on Constantine also defeated the eastern emperor Licinius and created a new capital of Christendom at Constantinople, on the site of the old city of Byzantium. As a result of Constantine's conversion to Christianity and his encouragement of it, persecution of the Christians ceased and they were even given respected positions of public trust. For the first time Christians worshipped openly, without fear, and their liturgy began to flower.

Saint Ambrose

◆

Particularly instrumental in both the development of the church and its music was Saint Ambrose (340–397), archbishop of Milan. An ecclesiastical statesman, he is credited with strengthening the Church against pagan and heretical beliefs and with asserting its power in religious matters over even the emperor himself. Ambrose introduced the singing of hymns and Psalms in an antiphonal manner, soloist versus congregation or congregation divided, into the Church of the west. He himself composed a number of hymns, some of which are authenticated and still in use today.

Saint Benedict of Nursia

◆

After the fall of Rome in 476, the Visigoths expanded into France and conquered Spain. Italy fell into the hands of a barbarian general, Odoacer, who got rid of the puppet emperors. Then barbarism took over in Western Europe. The Church remained virtually the only stable element in an otherwise confused and chaotic world. However, a bright light emerged during this period—Saint Benedict of Nursia—who, in 520, founded the famous monastery of Monte Cassino in southern Italy. There he formed the Benedictine order of monks, which bears his name. The *Rule for Monasteries*, composed by him for the instruction and schooling of the monks, reveals his concern with all aspects of life, from religious observance to the manual labor necessary to care for the community's physical needs. Particularly relevant to the history of chant is the fact that Benedict established the

Divine Office—eight services each day throughout the year. Note that he divided the day into an "octave" of services separated by seven intervals of various activities. Again we see how musical thinking informs, guides, and structures monastic life.

Pope Gregory I
♦

Pope Gregory I (*c.* 540–604), for whom the Western chant repertory has been named, was an energetic church leader in both civil and ecclesiastic matters and a prolific writer. It is doubtful that he was a composer or singer. In fact, it is said that at one point he actually reprimanded his deacons for singing the liturgy, saying that they would be better off preaching and caring for souls than winning praise for their voices. Gregory is often pictured as receiving chant music from the Holy Spirit, symbolized by a dove sitting on his shoulder and whispering into his ear. Whatever we know of his career would suggest that he was writing not music but biblical commentary.

Born into a wealthy, noble Roman family, Gregory received an excellent Latin education. Trained for a political career, by 573 he was prefect of Rome. However, inspired by the example of Benedict of Nursia, he resigned this position, gave away his inheritance, and founded a Benedictine monastery. Later in his life the Church again recognized his political and administrative talent by ordaining him deacon of Rome and papal ambassador to Constantinople. In 590 he was called to the papacy.

Gregory wrote voluminously and his influence was far-reaching. He was eventually declared Doctor (*i.e.,* "teacher") of the Church, a title shared with saints Ambrose, Augustine, and Jerome. It is unlikely that Gregory actually composed any of the chants that bear his name. Most probably they were not even written under his direct supervision, though some of them might have been developed under his authority. The repertory of Gregorian Chant as we know it today could never have been the work of just one person. Rather it is the result of an evolutionary and cumulative process extending over several centuries.

Gregory's main contribution was not work with music per se, but his ability to disseminate the Christian faith throughout the Roman Empire, even as far as Britain. For his many gifts as writer, diplomat, administrator, and man of faith, his name has been perpetuated over the years by association with Western chant.

The Diversification of the Liturgy

◆

From the sixth to the eighth century, while Islam was widely extending its religion and culture, the Latin world was falling into the Dark Ages. Urban civilization almost disappeared, and superstition held full sway. Only the Christian Church kept the light of culture burning by forming monastic communities where manuscripts were kept and copied and some of the learning stayed alive. Meanwhile several regional variations of the Christian liturgy had sprung up—Mozarabic on the Iberian Peninsula, Gallican in Gaul, Ambrosian in Milan, and Roman in Rome—each with its own particular flavor.

The Origins of Carolingian Chant

◆

There is ample historical evidence to indicate that, beginning with the reign of Pope Vitalian (657–672), the liturgical music of the papal court underwent a significant renewal. The chants had become overloaded with extraneous or passing notes (that is, intermediary notes added between existing notes). These tended to blur the melodic line, rendering it less clear. The pope and his court, who understood the vital importance of clarity in music, decided to remedy the situation. Under their influence and most probably with the help of Byzantine musicians, the chants were restored to something more akin to their ancient form. From these efforts came a renewed chant, remarkable in its rhythmic approach. The notes, rather than being light and of equal duration, were each long enough to be divisible into two short notes, a very sophisticated form of free rhythm, particularly well adapted to coincide with the accentual patterning of the Latin language itself. It was easy, for example, for the same melodic notes to accommodate *dó-mi-nus*, with its accent on the first syllable, or *lau-dá-te*, with its accent on the second. Each word received proper weight and emphasis because each syllable had its own sacred "acre" that might or might not be divided into two lots (or augmented by adding the lot next door).

This rhythm, sometimes called "proportional," was capable of great variety and provided considerable challenge to singers at the time. The more difficult passages would typically be sung by a cantor or soloist specially trained within the *scholae cantorum* or "singing schools."

In Rome itself the only place where the renewed chant was offered with any degree of regularity was in the pope's private chapel. On a few days of special celebration during the year, however, the pope and his court would travel to certain other churches throughout the city, where they would sing the new liturgical chant. The rest of the time they kept it to themselves while the general community of believers continued to hear only what they had been listening to for years.

If the status quo prevailed in Rome, it was not so north of the Alps. Pippin (or Pépin) the Short, king of the Franks from 751 to 768 and father of Charlemagne, expressed great interest in the reformed music. At his request, especially trained singers or cantors were sent from Rome north to Gaul to visit his court and teach the new music. The cities of Rouen and Metz were particularly receptive, welcoming the teachers from Rome who would train their monks.

King Pippin did much to spread the sound of the new liturgy, but it was his son, Emperor Charlemagne (reigned 768–814), who really seized upon the idea and transformed it into a mission. He saw in it the possibility of an exceedingly effective means of uniting his far-flung empire politically, culturally, and religiously by associating with it a sound reminiscent of the splendors of the Eastern Church at Byzantium. With encouragement from Charlemagne, Pope Stephen III agreed to send cantors to numerous places throughout Gaul. The cantors, apparently, had other ideas. Being Romans they resented the dominance of the Northern Franks and jealously guarded their monopoly on the new church music. Wanting to keep the singing of the liturgy under their exclusive control, they resisted with all their might the plans forced upon them and engaged in wholesale sabotage of the proposal. Their modus operandi was to vary their methods at each place, teaching the chant differently and incorrectly. The result of this plot was extreme confusion everywhere within the empire, a situation that was eventually perceived by Charlemagne himself, whose sensitive musical ear noticed the flagrant discrepancies as he traveled from city to city.

One has to recall the central importance of music in the world views of civilizations that preceded ours to appreciate the severity and depth of this action. The cantors were intent upon interfering with the very structure of the empire itself. Even in our days, imagine what would happen if the president of the United States decided to dispatch music teachers to every state of the Union to teach the national anthem (correctly) and all these teachers got together and decided to teach a different version in each state. Think of the confusion, phone calls, letters to the editor, not to speak of marches, countermarches, and violence in the streets that would ensue!

Eventually the perpetrators were punished, but the attitude of the *schola* did not change. Charlemagne finally solved the problem by sending two of his own clerics, incognito, to the papal court in Rome to receive the true instruction. These men were then dispatched to teach the new chant in the cathedral at Metz, whence it was spread—this time correctly— throughout Gaul.

This story, told by the ninth-century monk Notker, partly explains why so few Roman manuscripts of this early chant ever existed. Writing the music down would have forced consistency and would have made dissemination much easier, something that the papal *schola* resisted as long as it could.

How, then, are we able, more than a thousand years later, to ascertain the sophisticated rhythmical qualities of this music and have a good idea of how it might have sounded? The most reliable evidence comes from chant books that were written by scribes in the tenth century, notably in the churches at Laon, Chartres, and St. Gall.

Chant Books

◆

The chant books were used by conductors, presumably to refresh their memories before and perhaps during the actual performance; the singers did not need these books, since the chant resided in their minds and hearts and was drawn from them by the hand of the conductor. The books contained the liturgical text and, above each syllable, certain musical signs, which, normally, are not difficult to interpret. Here are some examples in Metz notation:

> ╱ the *tractulus,* from the Latin *tractus* meaning "drawn out,"
> is most frequently used and suggests a long, poised note;
> • the *punctum,* "point," indicates a short note.

Some of the musical signs also show the direction in which the melody is moving:

/ the *virga*, "green twig or rod," stands for one long note, higher than the preceding;

⌡ or ╱ the *podatus*, "foot," meant two short or two long notes ascending;

7 or ⌐ the *clivis*, "slope," indicated two short or two long notes descending.

Slightly more complicated configurations were:

√ the *porrectus*, "reached out," which represented two short notes and a long, in a high-low-high pattern; and

∧ the *torculus*, "wine press," the same, but low-high-low.

Occasionally in the text one finds small letters, which add further clarification, beside the musical signs: a tiny *t* for *tene*, "hold"; *a* for *auge*, "lengthen"; *c* for *celeriter*, "quickly"; *h* for *humiliter*, "lower"; and *eq* for *equaliter*, "same pitch as the preceding." We readily recognize in these Latin words the ancestors of the English words tenacious, augment, celerity, humility, and equality.

The fascinating thing about these musical signs is not simply the fact that they indicate the rhythm and contour of the melodic line but that they show the conductor the way his or her hand should move in the air while directing. When compared to later medieval manuscripts, these early chant books may seem rather less than precise. It must be remembered, however, that the singers were part of a well-developed oral tradition whereby the chants were learned by ear, never by looking at the written page. Melodies and their pitches were familiar, known by heart, and had only to be drawn forth from them by the conductor through the careful use of the hand.

One of the early chant manuscripts referred to as Laon 239, studied in depth in the 1950s by musical paleographer Jan Vollaerts and further clarified by Dom A. Gregory Murray, probably gives the best and clearest indication of how the "proportional" chant sounded, so much so that we ourselves can experiment with conducting and singing these short lines taken from it:

Vi- as   tu - as,   Do - mi - ne
"Your ways, Lord"

Remember that ⁄ *tractulus* indicates a long note, and that ⁊ *clivis* and ⌡ *podatus* each sign two short notes, descending in the first case and ascending in the second. Try this line as well:

Do- mi - ne   de - us   sa - lu - tis   me - æ
"Lord God of my salvation"

Start with a long, low note on *Do*, then divide *mi* evenly into *mi-i* while raising the pitch. Hold steady, long notes on *-ne de-us* and *sal-* and then divide *lu* into *lu-u* with the first syllable lower than the second. Hold steady on *-tis*. In singing the word *me-æ*, change from high to low shorts and give the final syllable *æ* a triple pulse *æ, æ, æ*—short, short, long. Perhaps you would find it easier to watch a conductor's hand!

It would be incorrect to assume that this early chant was sung in a rigid, mathematical way. Any single-line melody always reveals subtle variation in tempo and dynamics. However, historical evidence is abundant that the new chant, so favored by Charlemagne as a means toward religious, cultural, and political unity, did have a carefully thought-out, measurable but free rhythm.

The measured quality of the music can be appreciated in the hymn *"Tibi, Christe, splendor Patris,"* an early chant presented in the Episcopal Church's *The Hymnal 1982*, its rhythm reconstructed by the Schola Antiqua:

1 Al - le   lu - ia,   song of   glad- ness, voice of   joy   that
2 Al - le   lu - ia   thou re- sound-est, true Je - ru - sa -
3 Al - le   lu - ia   though we cher - ish and would chant for
4 There-fore in   our   hymns we pray thee, grant us,   bless - ed

can - not   die   al - le - lu - ia   is   the   an - them
lem and free;   al - le - lu - ia, joy - ful   mo - ther,
ev - er - more   al - le - lu - ia   in   our   sing - ing,
Trin - i - ty,   at   the last to   keep   thine Eas - ter,

ev - er   raised by   choirs on   high;   in   the house of
all thy chil - dren sing with thee;   but by Bab - y -
let us   for   a   while give o'er,   as   our Sa - vior
with thy faith - ful   saints on high;   there to thee for

God a - bid - ing thus they sing e - ter - nal - ly.
lon's sad wa - ters mourn-ing ex -iles now are we.
in his fast - ing plea - sures of the world for - bore.
ev - er sing - ing al - le - lu - ia joy - ful - ly.

This piece is regular, not free, but each note is given its own space and dignity in what is basically a calm, ordered progression. Listening to this kind of chant, one has the impression of walking very close to a line from which the music departs somewhat but to which it regularly returns. It is as if the music, rather than calling us to the far-flung reaches of heaven, is inviting us to remain right here where we are, moving along our spiritual path upon the earth. It calls us back to ourselves, to where we are, to a God who can be found in our own hearts.

Even in the following example, *"Ad te levavi,"* "To you I lift up my soul," which opens the Mass for Advent, where the rhythmical patterns are nonrecurring and much more complex than in the previous example, the effect of dignified walking is still present. Here we see the same rhythmic principle of longs and shorts in 2:1 ratio freely arranged accompanying a prose text that is very freely accentuated. So successful is this proportional rhythm, that the chant can even be translated into and sung in English with no discernible loss.

Ad te le-va-vi a- ni-mam me- am: de-us me-

us, in te con-fi- do, non e- ru- be-

scam; ne- que ir-ri- de- ant me

i-ni-mi- ci me-i: et- e- nim u-ni-ver-

si qui te ex- pe- ctant, non con-fun-

den- tur. ℣ Vi-as tu- as do-mi-ne de- mon-stra mi-hi,

et se-mi-tas tu - as do-ce me.   Ad   te...

To you I lift up my soul: in you, my God, I place my trust; do
not let me be ashamed; neither let my enemies exult over me: of
all those who wait for you, not one shall ever be disappointed.
Show me your ways, O Lord, and teach me your paths.

In this we are reminded of the French Romanesque
churches—not the tall, light-filled and soaring Gothic edifices
of the later twelfth century but the solid, rectangular, dark
churches of two centuries earlier, built to contain and retain the
divinity within their walls. The churches sit squarely upon the
earth and are firmly grounded in it. Both architecture and chant
proclaim the same spirituality: "Thy will be done on earth"—
which, of course, suited the emperor's purpose rather well.

There is in this rhythm a manly, almost militaristic quality
that has its parallel in the nearly contemporary development of
such chansons de geste as the "Song of Roland," which recounted
the proud deeds of valor of the Frankish knights battling the

Moors. That same song of Roland was said to have been sung at Hastings in 1066 as the troops of William the Conqueror lined up for battle against the English.

The proportional chant so admired by Charlemagne and practiced at his insistence throughout his empire, but particularly in the churches of Metz, Laon, Rouen, and St. Gall, reached its zenith in the tenth century and began to decline with the eleventh. A medium best suited to either a soloist or a small group of trained singers, the chant, with its complex rhythm, proved unsuitable for singing by poorly trained choirs. Also, with an increased number of offices and masses, as monasteries grew in size, quality may have been given over to quantity. The clear differentiation of long and short notes so essential to the earlier chant gradually gave way to a manner of singing that equalized the rhythmical value of the notes.

Cluny

◆

The Abbey of Cluny in Burgundy occupied a central position

in Christendom from its foundation in 910 throughout the whole medieval period. It finally took the French Revolution to destroy its power. The abbey was conceived as a totally independent institution under the leadership of its abbot, and neither bishops nor temporal powers could in any way interfere with its activities. It was directly linked with the Church of Rome and came into existence at a time when the centers of learning founded by the Carolingians in cathedrals and monasteries were in overall decline.

Under the leadership of a remarkable succession of abbots, Cluny's influence spread mainly over France and Spain. It was one of the principal contributors to the flowering of Romanesque art. Cleverly maintaining independence from the emperor, kings, and bishops, adhering to a strict rule, the Cluniac order became a beacon of reform in a church in which temporal power had come to corrupt the spiritual. Raoul Glaber, a monk and chronicler of the eleventh century, wrote:

> This convent has not its equal anywhere in the Roman world.
> . . . The very great number [400] of monks [allows] masses to
> be celebrated constantly from the earliest hours of the day

until the hour assigned for rest; and they go about it with so much dignity and piety and veneration that one would think they are angels rather than men.

This intense ritual activity, guided by a diligent striving for perfection, had a marked effect on the celebration of the Mass and the way music was sung.

Equalist Chant

◆

The measurable chant explained above contrasts markedly with the equalized chant that has been the interpretation used since the eleventh century. This style, sung beautifully by the monks of Santo Domingo de Silos, has a sweeter, more celestial, even ethereal quality, more in tune with the treading of angels than with earthbound wayfarers on the move, even to heaven. The change from one style to another had, no doubt, many causes, but it is significant that as this shift was taking place in liturgical music, vernacular literatures were developing. The whole concept of chivalry was being established, and courtly love

songs and poems were being created and disseminated by trou-
vères and troubadours, ambulant poets and minstrels who would
go from castle to castle singing their repertory. At this time also,
the cult of the Virgin Mary spread over Christianity, East and
West. There is indubitably a feminine quality to this new style
that contrasts it with the earlier proportional music, a quality
that can best be appreciated by listening to the Spanish monks
sing the *Ave mundi spes Maria*, "Hail the world's hope, Mary."

By the end of the twelfth century the chant repertory had so
greatly increased that it could no longer be committed to memory. The writing down of pitches became increasingly necessary,
and a new system of musical notation with squared-off musical
signs, sometimes referred to as *neumes*, placed on a four-line staff,
came into use. The neumes were relatively large and did not provide for any precise indication of rhythm. Moreover, innovative
musicians were focusing attention not so much on rhythmic
sophistication as on the development of polyphonic music, or
music of more than one part. Chants that had previously been
sung in unison now were enriched by the addition of other notes

CHAPTER 4

THE WAY OF DEVOTION

Private and Communal Worship

◆

The Church has always distinguished between private worship—the prayers, reading of scripture, and meditation that is carried out by individuals alone—and the liturgy, which is celebrated communally. Derived from a Greek word meaning "an act of the people," liturgy is the formal worship enacted by a religious community, coming together to offer thanks to God. The communal aspect is of the utmost importance, since it is not only the action of the priest or celebrant at the altar but also the collective intention and attention of the assembled body of worshippers that gives the liturgy its healing power.

Monastic Life and the Divine Office

◆

The monastery is the best place to understand the intimate connection of the liturgy with the events of everyday life. This sacred relationship is described in great detail by Saint Benedict in his *Rule for Monasteries.* No aspect of either individual life or life in community is left out of this short, very much to-the-point prescription for the Benedictine path to God. For this reason, *The Rule,* as it is familiarly known, has been the guide of this religious order throughout the centuries. Because the way that the Benedictine monks sing the chants is so intimately connected with their way of life, it is vital to examine the monastic setting.

The early monasteries provided modest, practical accommodation for about a dozen monks and their abbot. The buildings themselves demonstrated concern not only for the life of the spirit but also for the physical needs of the community. Not far from the church could be found the granary, the bakehouse, the brewhouse, the outhouses, and the infirmary. The monks slept in dormitories, studied and copied both scriptural texts and music in the scriptorium, and celebrated the daily Office and Mass in their church. Normally the monastery was surrounded by farmland, where the monks worked daily for about six hours, in addition to their daily three hours of spiritual reading and five hours of communal worship.

The central fact of monastic life was the *Opus Dei*, "The Work of God," which was the coming together at prescribed times for prayer and the praise of God. These periods are referred to as the Divine Office or the Canonical Hours. Saint Benedict speaks of seven offices in the day and one in the night. Eight times a day, then, the monks met to sing the Psalms, listen to scriptural readings, and offer prayers so that the presence of Christ, so strongly evoked in the Mass, was recalled and consciously maintained.

It is highly significant that there were seven services by day and one by night. We recognize in this number an octave (eight services separated by seven periods similar to the eight notes separated by seven intervals). As the movements of the celestial spheres obey the *musica mundana*, the daily life of the monks follows the *musica humana,* and their voices, the *musica instrumentalis.* As above, so below. Octave within octave, the same principles govern them all. The monks not only chant the music, but their very life becomes music within the universal symphony. In this there is no monotony. On the contrary, there is a melody with changes of intensity, pitch, and tone provided by the variety of activities—prayer, study, and labor. The changes of the hours of the day, by the clock and the Divine Office, as well as the changes of the seasons, both natural and liturgical, relate the octaves they experienced to the universal cycles.

One can observe, even today, that the churches in which the monks worshipped were designed in accordance with the same rules: the architectural proportions follow musical ratios, and in many cases the plan and elevation themselves show an organization governed by the octave. The building orientation, with its choir turned to the east, toward the rising sun, and its main entrance to the west, toward the setting sun, integrates the church with the cycle of time.

Coming back to the number seven, Saint Benedict himself

refers to the sacredness of this number which, in medieval numerology, stood for the union of heaven and earth, the three members of the Trinity—Father, Son, and Holy Spirit—meeting and dwelling in the four elements of the universe—air, fire, water, and earth. Furthermore, the number seven is seen in the seven-day cycle of the week, the seven planets, and the age of seven at which a child is said to attain the age of reason, the seven ages of man from birth to death, and so on.

The pattern of offices as prescribed by Saint Benedict was somewhat variable according to the season of the year. The office or service of Matins (Latin *matutina*, "morning"), having its origin with the Easter Vigil during which the faithful awaited the dawn of Christ's resurrection, took place during the night. In winter the monks arose to worship around two A.M., returning afterward either to scriptural study or to bed as they felt the need. In summer, however, the time for Matins was later, shortly before Lauds (Latin "praise"), the office that took place at sunrise. Benedict allows time between the two offices for the monks to take care of the "necessities of nature," but it is clear that he is eager to have both services expedited somewhat so as to have everyone out working on the land during the early hours of daylight.

Other obligatory opportunities for worship were provided by the hours of *Prime, Terce, Sext,* and *None* (Latin for "First, Third, Sixth, and Ninth"), offices that often took place around six A.M., nine A.M., midday, and three P.M. but were arranged according to the season. These "Lesser Hours" were followed by Vespers (from Latin *vespera,* "evening") at sunset and Compline (Latin *hora completa,* "completed hour") before retiring.

At each service the Psalms were sung, as prescribed by Benedict. He allowed a little flexibility, but his basic recommendation, quoted from *The Rule,* was that

> the full number of 150 Psalms be chanted every week and begun again every Sunday at the Night Office. For those monks show themselves too lazy in the service to which they are vowed who chant with less than the Psalter with the customary canticles in the course of a week, whereas we read that our holy Fathers strenuously fulfilled that task in a single day. May we, lukewarm that we are, perform it at least in a whole week!

In addition, and depending upon the particular hour, other music was chanted: hymns, which were poems of a devotional nature, more popular in sentiment than the Psalms and having more rhythmic appeal, and canticles, New Testament songs such as Mary's *Magnificat*, ("My soul doth bless the Lord, and my spirit rejoices in God my savior."). Passages of scripture were proclaimed and responses and prayers were sung.

The Celebration of the Mass
◆

However important a place the Divine Office occupied in the life of the monastery, it was the regular celebration of Mass that was the focus, the center upon which everything else turned. It is important to note that the Mass was traditionally viewed as experiential. In the Middle Ages members of the worshipping community did not attend services thinking that they would learn something new and different. In fact, for more than a thousand years it is unlikely that many could have understood very much of the Mass liturgy, since it was proclaimed in Latin, a language unfamiliar to most people. But whether they knew it or not, to the extent that they were willing participants, they were being acted upon by the very structure of the ceremonies. For, as explained in Chapter 2, the organization of the Eucharistic ceremony followed an octave, an orderly progression taking the participant through all the steps of an evolution from his or her entrance into the church to divine union with Christ. The prepared participant was therefore "tuned" by the ceremony and could not but respond through the grace of God like a string plucked by a skillful musician resonating to it. But it needed two fundamental ingredients at the critical moments: the faith of the participant and the absolute grace of God.

Rather than being an occasion for engaging the intellect, the Mass was a time for invoking the mysterious presence of God through acts of thanksgiving and praise. The traditional Christmas Mass therefore did not begin with the celebrant's telling the congregation, "Today we are going to be speaking about and remembering the birth of Christ." Instead, attention would immediately be drawn musically to the theme for the day: *"Puer natus est nobis, et filius datus est nobis: cuius imperium super humerum eius."* "A child is born to us, a son is given to us, his shoulders shall bear princely power." This musical introduction, called the Introit or entrance song, announced the particular theme of the Mass being celebrated on that day and brought the worshippers directly into remembrance of the spirit and intent of what was to follow.

The Introit, musically demanding and changing with each Mass, was normally sung by a small group of singers. From the beginning of the Mass an atmosphere was created in which all the senses were involved—listening to the music of sacred scripture, seeing the symbolic movements of the celebrant, tasting the bread and the wine offered at the Communion, smelling the incense used to purify the air, touching another person's hand or offering an embrace at the time when worshippers wished each other "the Peace of the Lord." The liturgy was an elaborately designed drama that proclaimed to worshippers not just the external story of the life of Christ but its inner meaning. Through the action of the Mass their lives were transformed in a profound and mysterious way.

The first part of the Mass was referred to as the Mass of the Catechumens, those studying the faith, and was similar in its readings and prayers to Jewish synagogue services. It began with the Introit followed by the Kyrie Eleison, a prayer asking for the mercy of the Lord, sung three times by the congregation. This was followed by the Gloria in Excelsis Deo, "Glory to God in the Highest," based on the song of the angels to the shepherds at the time of the birth of Jesus. Both the Kyrie and Gloria are part of the Ordinary, or unchanging part of the Mass, in other words the part that is said or sung each time the Mass is celebrated. Next came the Collect, a prayer sung by the celebrant and appropriate to the particular feast day of the liturgical year being celebrated.

With the Collect ended the entrance ceremonies, the *re* of our octave progression, the *do* being, in this case, the state of affairs before the start of the ceremony, the state of consciousness outside the church.

Next came the Service of Readings, the *mi* of the octave. It included readings from the Old Testament or the New Testament Epistles (letters written by the apostles of Jesus to the newly forming communities of faith). Before the actual reading of the Gospel (the life and teachings of Christ as revealed in the New Testament books Matthew, Mark, Luke, and John), there were several types of musical responses to the scripture already read, the Gradual (from the Latin *gradus*, "step"), so named because the cantor stood at the steps to the altar to sing it; the Alleluia or Tract, also sung by trained singers, the former a joyous song of praise, the latter a replacement used during times of penance or mourning. The Alleluia and the Tract, both part of the Proper or changing part of the Mass, tended to lengthen as time went on, becoming more and more elaborate. Also added was the Sequence, a hymn that was popular in nature and extended the Alleluia even more on certain feast days. The reading of the Gospel was optionally followed by a sermon. Then came the all important Credo (from the Latin *credo*, "I believe"), or statement of faith, sung by the congregation as part of the Ordinary, which concluded the Mass of the Catechumens.

This Credo makes the link to the Mass of the Faithful, which begins with a step corresponding to the *fa* in the octave progression. It is at the interval between *mi* and *fa* because it is the affirmation of faith that transforms the Catechumen into one of the Faithful and allows the octave to proceed normally. If the Credo cannot be sincerely uttered, the progression cannot take place.

The Mass of the Faithful which followed was liturgy whose purpose was to recall so deeply the life and sacrificial death of Christ that he was felt to be present with the worshippers. The shared presence of Christ was a powerful reminder that the crumb of bread and the sip of wine were being changed into his likeness and that this was also happening to all those present as they participated in the mystery.

> And the Word was made flesh and dwelt among us (and we beheld his glory, the glory as of the only begotten of the Father), full of grace and truth.   John 1:14

This most holy of moments was carefully prepared by the liturgy of the Offertory (marked in the octave progression by the note *fa*), a processional sung by the *schola* as the bread, wine, and other gifts, "the work of human hands," were brought to the altar.

This was followed by the Eucharistic Prayer, consisting of the *Praefatio*, "Preface," sung by the celebrant, and the *Sanctus*, "Holy, holy, holy," chanted by the congregation and providing a bridge to the *Canon*, "law," the most sacred, unchanging part of the Mass, read by the celebrant in a lowered voice while a profound silence was kept in the congregation. When the Canon was completed, everyone responded with a resounding *Amen*, "So be it," indicating approval and acclamation. The solemnity of this part of the Mass was emphasized by its place in the octave at *sol*, musically the dominant note. Following the Canon, the Communion Cycle started with the *Pater Noster*, "Our Father"— the prayer Jesus himself taught his disciples to say, offered by the celebrant. This corresponds to the note *la* of the octave.

Then the congregation sang the *Agnus Dei*, "Lamb of God," a prayer petitioning for mercy and peace, corresponding to the note *si*. Both Sanctus and Agnus Dei belonged to the Ordinary of the Mass.

The following step, the Communion, falls within the interval between *si* and *do*. It is the other critical step in the octave progression, filled only by divine grace. Without it, the progression cannot proceed. Here the participant may experience divine union. At the Communion a brief text or antiphon appropriate to the day, followed by a psalm, was sung by the *schola* while the worshippers processed to the altar to receive the elements.

Finally, at the conclusion, corresponding to the note *do*, the deacon (assistant to the celebrant) sang the words *"Ite missa est,"* "Go, you are dismissed," to which all the worshippers responded, *"Deo gratias,"* "Thanks be to God."

Another name for the Mass of the Faithful is the Eucharist. It is the time for giving thanks, the central purpose of the Mass. While the worshippers were participating in this thanksgiving, they were brought by the majesty and balance of the liturgy into a state of peace and unity, in which Christ's mysterious presence among them and within them became a living reality. For a few moments they experienced their essential oneness both with Christ and God.

By the year 1000 the Mass had taken shape as just described, and it continued to be celebrated in this way for more than 900 years, from Carolingian times to the Second Vatican Council in the 1960s.

As time went on the number of services greatly increased. Many new feast days in honor of particular saints or the Virgin Mary were added. Each time the physical remains of a saint were translated (carried) to a new resting place, there was an occasion for elaborate liturgy. A famous example of this was the installing of the body of Saint James at Santiago de Compostela in northwestern Spain, a cathedral that later became an important center of spiritual pilgrimage.

The liturgy was also expanding through the addition of tropes, which were either musical or textual additions to the existing chants, and liturgical dramas, plays that illustrated the content of the Proper for the day. Subjects that were often enacted were the birth of Christ, the visit of the Holy Magi, and the *Quem queritis*, "Whom are you seeking?," which depicts the angel at the tomb of Christ questioning the three women who had come to anoint his body on Easter morning. These liturgical dramas expanded from simple dialogues to full-length plays with scenery and costumes, but they always retained a sung rather than a spoken format.

The Liturgical Year

◆

The Divine Office and the Mass are important in and of themselves, but it is vital to see them as part of the always repeating liturgical year. The liturgical year consists of two cycles that run concurrently. The more important of these cycles, called the Temporal Cycle, includes the commemoration of the principal events in the life of Christ and the observance of all the Sundays of the year. This cycle has to be adjusted annually to accommodate the movable date of Easter and the fixed date of Christmas. It relates the church liturgy to the astronomical cycle and the zodiac and therefore acts as a bridge between the *musica humana* and the *musica mundana.*

The Temporal Cycle includes six seasons beginning with Advent, a four-week period of preparation and anticipation of the birth of Christ. The season of Christmas begins with the celebration of Christ's nativity on December 25 and continues through January 5. The third season, Epiphany, starts on January 6, the Twelfth Night after Christmas, and recalls the manifestation of the divine nature of Christ to the people of the world, represented by the three Wise Men who came from the East to worship him. Lent, the most solemn season of the Christian year, begins five and a half weeks before Easter. It is characterized by penitential practices and culminates in the recollection of Christ's death and burial on Good Friday and Holy Saturday. Easter, the most joyous festival of the year, celebrates the Resurrection of Christ. It takes place on the Sunday following the full moon that occurs on or next after the vernal equinox on March 21st. The season of Easter lasts for seven weeks (note again the number), after which time Pentecost begins, the recollection of the coming of the Holy Spirit to the apostles and disciples of Christ and the continued presence of the Holy Spirit throughout history.

The second cycle, called the Sanctoral Cycle, indicates days when saints, apostles, and martyrs are to be specifically remembered and their lives and deeds recalled. Whereas the Temporal

Old Testament prophets for the coming of the Messiah, mirrored in the dark, quiet Advent days of preparation; the joy of Christ's birth and the recognition of his identity repeated in their own lives as children were born and nurtured. Through the proclamation of the Gospel they learned of Christ's miraculous healing power and witnessed this at work within themselves. They relived Christ's triumphant reception in Jerusalem, followed all too quickly by the betrayal of his friends and his Crucifixion at the hands of the Roman authorities. In the Resurrection they saw, at the empty tomb but also in their own lives, the triumph of life over the powers of death. The Ascension, Christ's departure from them, was an absence that would enable his return to them at Pentecost in even greater power through the descent and subtly abiding presence of the Holy Spirit.

The season of Pentecost, the longest of the liturgical year, celebrated the joining of all the events of the life of Christ to the actual day-by-day experience of the worshippers. It was a point of meeting of liturgical and chronological time, where the Holy Spirit stepped into history, allowing for the imitation of

the proclamation of scripture were carried out without speaking, and each day the Great Silence was observed from the end of Compline until the end of Lauds. These periods of quiet, which were strictly enforced, provided space for each individual to look within both for forgiveness of sins and for the deepening assurance of God's immanent presence. They also helped the monks "to utter truth from the heart and mouth" when they did speak.

After Benedictines entered the monastery they were given a period of time to learn what would be expected. Their eventual vows required obedience to *The Rule*, to the directives of the abbot or abbess, and to the disciplines of the monastery, a promise to consider the way of life as revealed in the particular monastery as their personal way to God, and a willingness to develop and change according to the needs of the situation and the words of Christ who said, "Come, follow me." Obedience necessitated openness to hear instructions and a willingness to carry them out quickly and willingly. Benedict describes this state of attention and watchfulness when he speaks of how the monks were to sleep:

Let the monks sleep clothed and girded with belts or cords but not with knives at their sides, lest they cut themselves in their sleep—and thus be always ready to rise without delay when the signal is given and hasten to be before one another at the Work of God, yet with all gravity and decorum.

Upon entering the monastery, monks were asked to give up all of their personal possessions, conserving not even a pen or a pillow for themselves. They were also asked to surrender personal ambition and self-assertiveness, the desire to be different or to gain personal notoriety or distinction.

In exchange they received exactly what they needed to live—clothing, food, drink, writing materials, books—all in proper measure, not too much, but not too little either. Material things were given into their care but not their ownership. Because of this, each object, whether it was a chalice for the altar or a spade for the garden, received its fitting measure of respect and attention.

Saint Benedict speaks a great deal about the way the monks should live together as brothers in community. In the same way that material objects were all treated with equal concern and care, so each person was offered the same welcome and love. No difference was made between those with greater wit or intelligence and those with less, between those well provided with worldly talents and those less gifted. Competition was surrendered in favor of the absence of any kind of self-concern.

These principles of monastic life—attention to detail, listening, obedience, simplicity, economy, and, above all, unqualified love—are embodied in the singing and are transmitted by the chants.

CHAPTER 5

THE COMPOSITION AND NOTATION OF CHANT

Guido d'Arezzo and the Musical Octave

◆

There was in the first half of the eleventh century a dramatic musical innovation. An Italian musician and musical theorist, Guido d'Arezzo, had noticed a great deal of confusion in the singing of chants. Since there was no specific and universally recognized system of notation to write down the expanding repertory, the early monastic singers were probably left to "sing their own thing," referring at times to a few scratches on parchment, most often to their own shaky memory of the notes.

Guido sought to remedy the situation by inventing a system of squared notation with lines and spaces that could be used to indicate the pitches of the notes in the chants. The musical system used by Guido and his singers dates back to the ancient Greeks. The Greek names of the notes have been lost, but at some point Latin names were assigned.

To teach this system so that singers could remember relative pitches more easily, Guido employed a hymn in honor of Saint John the Baptist that was composed in the latter part of the eighth century. Each of its first six sections begins on a new note of the scale, and the syllable assigned to each of these notes became the name of that note (with *ut* being another word for *do*):

Eleventh-century hymnal from Munich; in *Monumenta Monodica Medii Aevi, I: Hymnen* ed. Bruno Stäblein, Kassel 1956.

That thy servants may freely proclaim the wonders of thy deeds, absolve the sins of their unclean lips, O Holy John.

It is important to understand that, by memorizing the song, singers also memorized the pitches of the successive notes with respect to each other and their placement on the staff. Apparently, with his new system Guido was able to produce a competent singer in one or at the most two years, whereas previously ten years of study had not been enough. The great change was that singers could now read and perform a melody that they had never before heard.

The Medieval Church Modes

◆

Much of Western chant is sung in a manner or mode that may be quite unfamiliar to our ears. The chants are based on eight-note scales as music is today, but these scales sound strange because of a different arrangement of whole and half tones. These eight modal scales were sometimes called by Greek names, although they were not the same as the ancient Greek modes. To avoid confusion, in medieval church music they are normally given the Roman numerals I to VIII. Since the classification took place only after the time of Guido, when more than 3,000 chants were already in use, it was done somewhat after the fact, and not all chants fit into a particular mode, although most do.

It is not easy for us to know right away what mode we are hearing. Experienced musicians can recognize certain melodic formulas that are characteristic in each case. Most important in identifying the mode is not the note on which the music starts, but the one on which it ends. The melody often returns to this *final* both at the end of a musical phrase and at the end of the piece itself. The final note determines the actual mode that is used in the chant, its particular arrangement of tones.

To gain a sense of this system it may be useful to spend a moment with the piano, since this instrument can provide a visual image as well as the approximate sound of what we are referring to. Begin by playing *do*, the note to the left of any two black notes, and continue for seven more white notes, so that you have listened to the whole octave:

do re mi fa sol la si do

Looking again at the piano, notice that between *mi* and *fa* and between *si* and *do* there is no black note. These are steps, called halftones or semitones, that are perceived by the ear as being less than a tone apart, while the others are a whole tone apart. The semitones and the whole tones sound very different.

To hear a modal scale, the one most often used in medieval chant, begin by playing or singing *re*, the note between the two black keys, and then continue, again ignoring the black keys, for seven more notes:

re mi fa sol la si do re

Notice that in this modal scale the position of the halftone interval has shifted so as to be placed between the second and third and the sixth and seventh notes creating, this time, a scale wherein the intervalic pattern established by the first four notes of the scale—whole tone/halftone/whole tone—repeats itself. Continue this procedure beginning first on *mi*, then on *fa*, and finally on *sol*. Each time start with the note and continue upward for seven more notes, ignoring the black keys:

mi fa sol la si do re mi
fa sol la si do re mi fa
sol la si do re mi fa sol

It should be remembered in doing this practice that because of the tempering of the piano, the sound will not be quite accurate. It will, however, suffice to give an idea of the sound of modal scales I, III, V, and VII, beginning on *re, mi, fa,* and *sol* respectively. These four scales are called "authentic," meaning that the *final* note is the lowest or next-to-lowest note in the chant.

The other four modes, numbered II, IV, VI, and VIII, are actually based on modes I, III, V, and VII, but the range of the melody is different, placing the *final* note in the middle rather than at the bottom of the range of the melody.

The ancient Greek modes were said to create very specific moods in the persons who listened to them. The story is told that, in the sixth century before the Common Era, a Greek youth, overwrought by listening to one of the modes, and learning that a rival was keeping company with his girlfriend behind closed doors, was about to set fire to the house where they were staying. When Pythagoras, philosopher and musical theoretician, heard of this, he had the offending mode stopped and, by using another, restored the youth to calm.

Although it is difficult to establish specific connections with the medieval church modes and certain moods or states of mind, it is apparent that certain subjective correlations are used by Gregorian composers. Dom Joseph Gajard, a monk at Solesmes (quoted by Dom Jacques Hourlier in *Entretiens sur la spiritualité du chant grégorien*, Solesmes, 1985) speaks of "the peaceful mode on *re*, the ecstatic *mi*, the refreshing *fa*, and the enthusiastic *sol*." In the hands of experienced chant composers, the modes were one of the tools used to present a particular "reading" of the text, giving to it the emotional quality required by tradition. For example, *Veni, sancte spiritus* "Come, Holy Spirit," is in Mode I—the peaceful mode on *re*—because, according to the tradition, it is through the Holy Spirit that Christ sends his peace, whereas *Lætatus sum*, "I rejoiced," is in Mode VII—the enthusiastic mode on *sol*.

The Relationship Between the Words and the Music

◆

The Latin language, in which all Gregorian Chant is sung, is particularly well suited for melody. The vowels and diphthongs are open and clear, making them easy to sustain. Words are generally divided into syllables ending in a vowel. The classical language required vowels to be either long or short, and the length of the vowels determined the stress pattern of the word. The accent was on the penultimate (next to last) syllable if the vowel were long, and on the ante-penultimate (before the penultimate) if the vowel were short:

Et vī dĭ- mŭs glō- rĭ - am ē- ĭus

And we saw his glory

By the third century the prominence of one syllable over the others remained a characteristic feature of the language, but this was determined not so much by length as by stress, or stronger expulsion of breath. In the earliest chants the purpose was to sing the lines as they were spoken, preserving the accent. In later chants it sometimes happens that the correct pronunciation of the Latin word is not respected and the music stresses the wrong syllable, making it less comprehensible.

Manuscripts from the eighth to tenth century indicate only the number and length of notes and ornaments and whether the melody goes up or down. However, as time went on, indications of pitch were increasingly shown. Square or diamond-shaped neumes were placed on a staff of from one to four lines scratched or inked on parchment; in many cases the lines are no longer clearly visible on the manuscript. Later the lines were drawn in color, usually red for *fa* and yellow or green for *do*. The clef, written at the beginning of the staff, gave the name and place of the notes placed on it. There were two clefs in use, the *do* clef, two dots, one above and one below the line indicating the position of *do*, and the *fa* clef, a note with descending tail followed by two dots, marking the place of *fa*:

do clefs   fa clefs

Both of the clefs were movable: the *do* clef was placed sometimes on the second line, often on the third line, and very often
on the top line. The *fa* clef was generally on the third, sometimes
on the top. The shifting of the clef was merely to enable melodies
of different range to be written on the staff without adding more
lines, thus conserving precious parchment.

With regard to the square notes themselves certain conven-
tions apply: Notes in ligatures were read from left to right, and
two notes aligned vertically were read from bottom to top.

Neume   Modern Equivalent   Neume   Modern Equivalent

We tend to think of later Gregorian Chant as smooth, the
melody progressing gently up and down the scale. When there
are melodic intervals or jumps, they are generally not large and
phrases gently rise upward from the *final* and fall back to it. A

skip of one note is the most common interval, with jumps larger than five notes quite rare—meaning that, when they do occur, they increase the dramatic effect. This can easily be heard at the beginning of the Introit *"Puer natus est,"* where the music jumps from *do* to *sol* on the word *"Pu-er,"* making the word sound much brighter than if the melody had changed from *do* to *mi* or *do* to *fa*.

P   U-er   ná – tus   est   nó – bis

The simplest way for the melody to be related to the text is one note for one syllable. Frequently, however, a syllable is set to two or more notes:

De – us   Chris – tus   glo – ri – a   ter – ra

It was not uncommon to have many notes—up to 100, for example—sung on a single syllable. All these notes taken together are referred to as a melisma. Here are examples:

ó-mnis   tér-   ra

Behind this greatly elaborated chant was probably the composer's desire to show off a little. However, it must be remembered that the amount of length and decorative melisma allowed
was always subject to the functional requirements of the liturgy.
Music for the Gradual and for the Alleluia sung between the
scriptural readings became more elaborate because time was available in the liturgy for listening and meditation.

The Abbey of Solesmes

◆

Much of the transcription of early chants has been accom-
plished at the Benedictine monastery of Saint-Pierre de Solesmes
in France. Dating back to the eleventh century, but destroyed
during the French Revolution, the monastery was founded again
in the 1830s by Dom Prosper Guéranger, a man who was pas-
sionately committed to restoring authentic chant melodies.

The first chant book was completed at Solesmes in 1856

after which many brilliant scholars of liturgy and church history joined the effort. During the last quarter of the nineteenth century the paleographers of Solesmes strove diligently to receive the Vatican's official acceptance of the work, which finally occurred in 1904. Today the work continues and visitors from all over the world go to Solesmes to hear the glorious music that is the result. One of Solesmes's greatest legacies has been the publication of *Paléographie musicale,* a series of books photographically reproducing major chant manuscripts from the tenth through the thirteenth century.

On the *Chant* recording, the chant moves lightly and smoothly, never slowly. The monks of the monastery of Santo Domingo de Silos are singing chant in the manner of the Abbey of Solesmes. The notes are basically all equal in length, and indivisible. Some may be lengthened a little and some shortened, nuanced so that one syllable is brought out more than another. Because this chant's rhythm was not measurable it has, from the thirteenth century, been called *cantus planus,* "plainchant" or "plainsong." The simpler word "chant" used throughout this book is broad enough to encompass the ancient metrical hymns, the free proportional chants of the ninth- and tenth-century manuscripts, and the equalist or plainchant tradition heard since the eleventh century.

The Gothic, arched movement of equalist chant may be understood in terms of twos and threes. Rather than signing each note, the conductor describes lesser and greater arcs in the air with his or her hand. A small circular movement of the hand encompasses two notes, a larger movement encompasses three notes, and thus with careful direction, called *cheironomy*, the singers are able to sing with one voice.

It is amazing that simple melodies, contained mainly within a range of eight notes, and having no beat or regularly repeating rhythmical pattern, were the indispensable accompaniment of the liturgy for hundreds of years. Perhaps it was their very simplicity that was partly responsible for their extraordinary resilience. In them modest musical means are used to enhance but never to steal attention away from the fullest expression of the Word, the Holy Scripture itself.

CHAPTER 6

THE WAY CHANT IS SUNG

The Sound of the Voice

◆

The human voice is a magnificent instrument. It is such an intimate part of us, so characteristically and personally our own, that friends are able to identify us on the phone after we speak little more than a single syllable. The sound of the voice can be very comforting and consoling, but it can also tear us apart. We may engage in conversation for many reasons: to entertain or be entertained, give or receive information, exercise our will, find companionship and support; however, more is always taking place than we are generally aware of. Especially when we are ill or when we are lonely, the actual content of what is said is not nearly so important as the sound. "Talk to me," we say, half jokingly, knowing deep within ourselves that the speaking itself is something that nourishes. When a friend speaks to us in a voice that is gentle, encouraging, and supportive, this can have a tremendous restorative effect.

In the sound of the voice we find a rich source of information that we often miss as we focus on the content of the conversation. Indeed, it is common for people to say the opposite of what they mean: "yes" when, in truth, it is "no." The words say that they agree, that they are ready to begin the project. The sound of the voice conveys their self-doubt, their hesitation, their reluctance to engage and get started. "How are you?" we ask. "Fine" is the response and, if we care to linger, we may find out that there is more to the story. "But you *said* . . . !" is our cry, after the fact. Understood, but too late, is "But you *really meant* . . ."

The voice is the barometer of our physical, emotional, and mental condition. It reveals our state of health and our amount of available energy; it holds the reservoir of our emotional life, indicating our present feelings and attitudes in general, and in the particular situation in which we find ourselves. It also retains, to a certain degree, what we have experienced in the past. From the sound of the voice comes information about our general alertness and intelligence. It tells if we are quick to process and move on or if we are more reflective and take our time in thinking about things. It tells the type of company, intellectual and social, that we keep. In short, the voice is a repository of everything that we have acquired, from our most persistent habits to our highest aspirations.

In addition to pitch and volume, the voice has speed and measure. Some people speak very quickly, with thoughts tripping and overlapping. It takes others much longer just to get the message out. Each sound has, also, its timbre, which is its own particular quality distinguishing it from all other sounds. These qualities are all variable and subject to change in accordance with our inner mental, emotional, and physical states.

Listening
◆

Now and again we pay attention to the sound itself, allowing it truly to inform us about what is going on behind the words. Listening to the sound of someone's voice, like listening itself, is a subtle effort. It is not the actual listening that is difficult, since listening is basically a passive activity. It is rather the effort needed to focus our attention on the sound and not to be distracted by our own thoughts or things that are happening nearby. If we are interested in what is being said, this is easier. If the conversation seems boring and tedious, we are ready to tune out and think about topics that we find more interesting or personally stimulating. At times it is difficult, especially when we are overwhelmed by all that we have to do, to stop our own activity and give listening the attention that it deserves. We keep on with the busyness, while the other person is speaking to us, with the result that we hear neither content nor sound accurately but, rather, a kind of faint echo on the periphery of our minds. It is no wonder that conversations like this are lost to memory, and errors creep into the work we were trying to accomplish while the other person was talking.

True listening requires presence of mind and a measure of

quiet in the head. People who engage in a daily practice of meditation find that such a discipline is helpful in providing a platform of silence with which to approach the day. Those who have come upon Gregorian Chant find that it, also, has the effect of opening the listening and stilling the mind. A little quiet is needed in order to stay with this kind of music in the first place. More quiet comes about as a result of continuing to avail ourselves of it.

The opening up and out of listening is important for our health and well being. There is a strong tendency on the part of most people to become completely absorbed in certain thoughts in their heads, sometimes even to the point where these fixed ideas induce a pathological state of mind. The simple exercise of sitting quietly, with straight and comfortable posture, and becoming aware of all audible sounds as they present themselves, is helpful in this regard.

Begin with sounds that are close by in the room where you are sitting and slowly expand the attention to encompass a steadily widening area—the whole house, the surrounding neighborhood, the community. Do not set up boundaries as to how far you may be able to hear. Do not let commenting on the experience detract from the actual listening. This simple effort of paying attention and remaining quite still will have the effect of opening up space in the mind. Having this space available at will is useful both in informing ourselves about the world and in listening to Gregorian Chant.

Hearing Our Own Voice

◆

In speaking or singing we can feel very vulnerable. Without necessarily understanding how it takes place, we are aware that the voice reveals a great deal about us. Fearing that the voice will expose too much—more than we want other people to know about us—we hold it back when we speak, causing the sound to stop only a few feet in front of our noses. Sometimes we refuse to use it altogether and actually remain silent in situations where speech would be a helpful gift to someone else. Even after years of performance, many professional lecturers or singers still experience twinges of anxiety before going on stage. The mouth goes dry and the legs tremble.

So great and so apparently normal is our identification with our own voice that we are especially sensitive to any criticism about it, especially when we are young. It is a sad fact that countless adults confess that they are unable to sing a note. They attribute this inability to perform what should be a natural and joyous activity to being told as children that they had no singing voice, should not participate but only mouth the words—worse, that they would ruin everything for the group if their voices were audible. These painful impressions of early childhood often go deep and are very far-reaching and damaging in their effect, so much so that people may be permanently prevented from ever attempting to sing.

Most of us do not listen closely to the sound of our own voices as we speak or as we sing. We have this pointed out to us most clearly when we realize that we no longer remember what we have just said! Perhaps we are racing, jumping ahead of ourselves in the mad dash to "get it all out." Maybe we are distracted by all the ideas, bright and otherwise, that bombard us on a more or less continual basis. It might also be that we feel we would hear in the sound of our own voice things that we are unprepared to hear. In any case, and for whatever reason, we find that we are not really listening to our own sound in the moment of speaking. We hear it on the rebound, as it were, and with a certain delay, if we hear it at all. If *we* are not willing to listen to the sound of our own voice, why should anyone else bother to listen to it?

Purifying the Sound and the Heart

◆

Just by listening to the sound of one's own voice it is easy to "get behind" the sound and unite with it. In this regard the practice of singing or toning simple vowels such as A (ah), I (ee), and U (oo), gently and easily on any comfortable pitch can help. As we sing and continue to listen to the sound we are making, we will notice that it changes. The amount of extraneous noise surrounding the sound gradually disappears and the note becomes clearer, purer, and more beautiful. There is increased awareness of what is being sung, a brightness and alertness that was not so apparent before. The sound becomes alive because there is someone present observing it and caring for it.

Eastern spiritual teaching says that certain sounds called mantras have the power, through their repeated utterance or chanting, to clear the mind of its superficial layers of thought—such as what I'm having for breakfast, what kind of car I'm going to buy, what movie I'd like to see—making it more receptive to the inner promptings of the spirit. In the context of Christianity, the repeated singing of the words of the Psalms is understood to have this same effect, giving the mind respite from its habitual meanderings and penetrating to the inner realm of the heart, where even the intentions and will may be purified.

Conscious Listening

◆

Since attentive, fine listening is somewhat of a lost art, even more should be said about it before we can turn our attention easily to the singing of chant. Good listeners do not turn on and off at will, shutting out what they think they do or do not want to hear. They consider this kind of voluntary deafness a high-risk activity that leads to missing not only important surface information but also the inner meaning of what is going on. They do not consider someone's speaking to them as an interruption, an intrusion into some sort of predetermined agenda that they have already established. Rather they view it as an opportunity to serve not only the person asking for their attention but the whole creation by engaging in a conscious rather than a mechanical activity. Doing this requires faith that the listening itself is worth the effort, that there will, in fact, be time to take care of all the other pressing concerns. It is, ultimately, the gift of ourselves and our time, in unselfish service to someone else.

Spiritual teaching has always pointed to the fact that everything in creation has a sound, its own unique vibration. As conscious listeners we may perceive more and more of what the universe is saying to us by the simple act of listening. We can learn to appreciate each and every sound—the chirp of the first July cricket, the whir of the booting computer, the calls of chil-

without undue vocal vibrato. The unadorned quality of the music lends itself to single-minded focus of attention, to full and undistracted participation in the act of worship that it embodies.

Within the Western Church chanting has not been limited to monastic settings. From the very beginning it was part of congregational worship in parish churches and cathedrals as well. All continued to use it until the sweeping changes following Vatican II. *The Hymnal 1982* of the Episcopal Church retains a number of these chants for its worship services.

There is no need for the monks or nuns to be professional singers. In fact, it is preferable for them to be without the vocal accoutrements that characterize the cultivated, artistic voice. In their singing is a sense of measure governed not by the individual and his vocal expertise but by the united effort of the group as a whole. It is important for everyone to sing the same pitch, breathe in the same place, sustain vowels, and articulate final consonants in a united and timely way.

Practice and training are needed, and in some cases it can be as long as four years before novices are ready for full participation. They must learn to listen not only to the musical notes but to the spaces between them. They must learn to make a resonating cavity not just of the mouth and throat but of the whole body. Since the lines of scripture to be sung are sometimes quite long, the singers must be capable of sustained control of the breath. For all of these requirements, posture must be straight.

The foundation of the chant is the daily *lectio divina* (reading of holy scripture), which is an intrinsic part of the religious life. The purpose is not to read at length, but in depth. A short passage is selected, often from the Psalms or the Gospel. The practice may be done alone or with a group. At first it is necessary to read the chosen lines slowly and carefully a number of times. If this is done silently, the words are repeated to oneself almost syllable by syllable. At first the texts are treated as subjects of conversation, each passage asking for a personal response. Interpretations and applications arise in the mind, and are then either spoken aloud or reflected upon inwardly. At no point is argument or dispute allowed; whatever comes about as a result of the reading is gratefully received and the process continues. As familiarity with the passage increases, the reader is led, more and more, to an experience of prayer. No longer a purely intellectual undertaking wherein one speaks with the characters involved, takes part in the drama, or relates and applies the teaching, the reading begins to affect the heart, the deepest seat of the emotions. It takes on more of the quality of a direct encounter with God or Christ. As faith and trust develop, the fruit of continual practice, the reading increases one's ability to rest in the presence of God, far beyond any concepts, feelings, or particular acts. These results remain even when one is in the midst of tremendous activity. For the singing monk or nun, intellectual acquaintance with the text is not the only thing to be desired; rather, it is the living experience, the realization within the self, of the passage that best informs the singing of it. Monastic life allows time not just for reading the holy words but also for their inner digestion and integration: the interiorization of the word of God.

In Benedictine monasteries a rule of silence is observed, whereby the community refrains from speaking for all or part of the day. The object of this discipline is to bring about an atmosphere in which controlling the tongue is less of a problem and full attention can be given to the singular purpose: that God's immanent presence become a living reality. The prevailing quiet provides a background for the singing of chant. It is a palpable presence before, during, and after the sound.

The Purpose of the Chant
◆

In every event, whether it is hammering a nail, caring for a young child, or playing a musical instrument, there is not simply the person who is carrying out the activity and the person or things being worked upon, there is also a hidden or third factor that will determine the quality of what is taking place. In the case of singing, there are the singers and the song. The third factor joining the two is the attitude of the singers, their personal and intimate response in the moment to the music. They may care deeply about what is going on, they may be indifferent, or they may be somewhere in between. In any situation people may be distracted, interested in personal gain, desirous of receiving something for themselves, or simply giving attention to the matter at hand.

The singing of Gregorian Chant requires a very calm, clear third point. This type of devotional music begs for complete anonymity on the part of the singers—a willingness to surrender all personal concerns, at the very least during the chants. Any lack of attention to the music, words, or breath, any stray thought or distraction, will be audible and will detract from the worship experience. The singing demands total presence of mind, total absence of self-concern, total obedience to the divine will as revealed in the exigencies of the music. Those of little faith may not be ready for this sort of experience.

Each time Gregorian Chant is sung it is first and foremost an act of obedience and faith. The music is there to be sung, not interpreted or embellished. The aim is to praise God through the musical expression of holy scripture. Singers report an experience akin to God singing through them rather than their singing to or for God. Through music they are brought to clearer remembrance of their divine source.

The Effect of the Chant

◆

The practical effect of this music is that it bears the mark of absolute anonymity. It is as if there is no actual singer, and yet the music itself is full of presence. During the singing, time seems to stop and the darting mind falls still and attentive, arrested from its worldly concerns and preoccupations. The sound itself is rich and full and yet, in some way, unobtrusive. It embodies all the elements of the universe itself. It is wide open as the ether or space in which it rests and is supported, and palpable as the gentle summer air touching our faces. With each phrase it is sent forth from silence and returns to silence, carried on the wave of the breath. Like fire, each line has its own brightness and energy, a force that is called forth, raised, and then surrendered. Like water, the music rises and falls in a gentle wave of love that bathes, cleanses, and caresses our spirits, leaving us buoyed up and restored. Like the smell of the earth overturned before planting, it is fresh and sweet, a gentle balm for our spirits.

CHAPTER 7

HEALING THROUGH CHANT

The Energy of Sound

◆

There is a story told by French physician and internationally renowned ear specialist Dr. Alfred Tomatis in an interview with Canadian writer and radio producer Tim Wilson. Dr. Tomatis visited a Benedictine monastery in France just after the Second Vatican Council in the early 1960s, when there was some discussion as to whether the Latin language should be retained for daily worship or whether the vernacular French, which was encouraged by the Council, should be adopted. Also under consideration was whether chanting should be continued or abandoned in favor of other activities thought to be more useful. The final outcome was the elimination of chant from the Divine Office.

Before long a change took place in the community. Monks who previously had been able to survive rather well on the customary three or four hours of sleep a night became extremely tired and prone to illness. Thinking that too little sleep might be the cause of their malaise, the abbot allowed more, but this did not help. The more the monks slept, the more tired they became. Even a change in diet was attempted—to a meat and potatoes regime, after vegetarianism had been the rule of the community for 700 years—but this too had no positive result.

The situation grew worse and worse until February 1967 when Dr. Tomatis was invited back to the monastery again to see if he could help with the problem. In the same interview Dr. Tomatis recalls that, when he arrived, "seventy of the ninety monks were slumping in their cells like wet dish rags." Upon examination, he found that the monks were not only tired but their hearing was not as good as it should have been. His solution to the problem was to use a device called the Electronic Ear to increase the monks' auditory sensitivity over a period of several months. The Electronic Ear, developed by Tomatis, is a cybernetic device with two channels joined by a gate which gives the patient sounds as normally heard on one side and, on the other side, the same sounds filtered to allow an improved audition, particularly of high frequencies. Changing channels from one side to the other exercises the muscles of the inner ear and makes it possible for the patient to regain auditory acuity and sensitivity. The other aspect of Dr. Tomatis's treatment was to have the daily chanting brought back immediately into the life of the monastery.

Within nine months the monks had experienced an extraordinary improvement, both in their ability to hear and in their general sense of health and well-being. Most were able to return to the way of life that had been normal in their community for so many hundreds of years—the extended periods of prayer, short nights of sleep, and the demanding schedule of physical work.

What had happened? Continuing the interview with Mr. Wilson, Dr. Tomatis went on to explain the vital role played by the ear in stimulating the brain's activity; in particular, it serves to

range. High frequencies in British English are due to the number of plosive sounds and the generally clipped way of speaking.

Dr. Tomatis points out that putting an oscilloscope to the sounds of Gregorian Chant reveals that it contains all the frequencies of the voice spectrum, roughly 70 to 9,000 hertz, but with a very different envelope curve from that of normal speech. The monks sing in the medium range—that of a baritone—but due to the unity and resonance of the sound, their voices produce rich overtones of higher frequency. It is these high tones, mainly in the range of 2,000 to 4,000 hertz, that provide the charge to the brain. When the monks referred to earlier were not chanting, they were missing their daily dose of energy. It is not difficult to understand the feeling of fatigue that they experienced.

These energies are very small in measurable terms. This is why they are often thought of as being of a subtle nature. The fact is that it is not their energetic content (*i.e.*, the quantity of watt-seconds, ergs, or any other measure we may care to use) that is important, but the information they carry. To draw a simple analogy: It is not the power of the signal sent millions of miles away to a space probe that matters so much as the shape of the energy that carries the information that operates a device or sends a series of pictures back to earth.

The way the monks receive energy through the sound is that it acts partly as a signal which, through the complex organization of the body and its energy fields, serves to reorganize the energy distribution within the body. The result is a sense of gaining energy or losing energy, depending on how these energies are redistributed within the centers.

From the point of view of the listener there is one further point to be made. We receive energy from listening to the chant but at the same time experience calm and tranquillity. This is due to the fact that we can participate in the same pattern of deep and peaceful breathing as the monks or nuns chanting the long, melismatic lines of Gregorian Chant. Most texts and melodies for Gregorian Chant can be found in the *Liber Usualis*, the Benedictines' daily song book. Many texts can also be found in any Missal or Breviary published before the Second Vatican Council in the early 1960s. Unfortunately, these books are no longer in print. However, if you can find a copy of the *Liber Usualis*, try singing along with a recording. As Tim Wilson says:

> Even if you read only enough music to discern that the melody rises or falls somewhat from note to note, you'll be surprised to find that it is as if you were singing in precisely the same time, at the same moment, as the voices you hear on the recording. A minor miracle of simultaneity, this—a manifestation of the losing track of time which Tomatis describes as characteristic of Gregorian.

Attention and Sound

♦

One of the most powerful ways that sound acts upon us is to draw us into itself. Some music holds our attention, allowing us, for a few moments, to merge with it completely. If we are closely attentive to the sound, we are taken into it, away from pain, sorrow, agitation, or confusion. Those familiar with meditative practice will recognize the same effect when they listen to and follow the sound of their sacred word or mantra. Through listening, the mind becomes centered and focused. We are no longer at sixes and sevens with ourselves, darting from one thought or bodily sensation to another. We may even find that, as a result of our entering more and more deeply into the center of the sound, our body straightens and we are more comfortable sitting right where we are. The sound holds us in a calm, safe place, one that we are loath to leave. It is as if there is no difference between the listener and the song; both are partaking of the same unity. When this happens, time seems to stop. No longer aware of past or future, we experience only the fullness of the present moment.

During attentive listening to chant, a balancing of body and mind occurs naturally, the direct result of the suspension of all but the gentlest of efforts required to maintain attention on the sound. A profound feeling of peace comes over us.

Music and sound are a form of subtle nourishment, for we are fed not only by food, but also by air and impressions. Digestion, breathing, and the processing of impressions are strongly interconnected. Balance between these functions results in the proper distribution of energy to the appropriate centers.

The efficient use of food within the body is obviously dependent on the oxygen brought in by the respiratory system. Equally important is the effect of sense impressions on the operation of both digestion and respiration. Even ordinary language acknowledges this link when we say that a certain impression takes our breath away or whets our appetite. One important element of good health is the maintenance of a suitable balance between these functions. The singing of chant requires the fine regulation and coordination of breathing and listening. When we listen to chant we fall easily into its rhythm and partake of these benefits.

The Effect of Sound
◆

It is often said that we live in a visual culture. The fact remains that we also live in a strongly sonic atmosphere. Canadian music professor and sound researcher R. Murray Schafer conducted an experiment with students from the United States, Canada, and Germany and other European countries. He asked each student to become deeply relaxed and then spontaneously recall and sing the note that came most naturally. For American and Canadian students this note was a B-flat, whereas for the Europeans it was G-sharp. Interestingly enough, in America and Canada electricity operates on an alternating current of 60 cycles per second, which relates to the B-flat; in Europe it is 50 cycles per second, connecting musically to the G-sharp.

We lose awareness of this background of sound. Nevertheless we are continually subjected to its humming coming from electronic devices: computers, lights, amplifiers, motors, and the like. In addition, we hear all sorts of loud noises—sirens, buses, airplanes, motors, and lawnmowers, not to mention boom boxes and music blasting from car windows. The American Speech and Hearing Association has estimated that 40,000,000 Americans live, work, or play around music that is dangerously loud. It is well documented that significant loss of hearing results when music is played too loud or too close to the ear. What we listen *to* matters. This is becoming more and more obvious.

Indeed, sound literally matters. It has the power to give shape to materials. The Swiss physicist Hans Jenny performed a number of stunning experiments illustrative of the effect of sound on inert matter. He placed substances such as iron filings, drops of water, soap bubbles, and lycopodium powder (spores of club moss) on a diaphragm and subjected them to a variety of sounds. As the sound changed, the result was a series of flowing, changing patterns of great beauty and complexity, which have been recorded and are shown in Professor Jenny's videotapes and two-volume presentation entitled *Cymatics* (the science of the way the properties of a medium change under the influence of vibration).

The effect of sound on living organisms is also well documented. Studies done in India by Dr. S. K. Bose and reported in *The Secret Life of Plants* by Peter Tompkins and Christopher Bird (HarperCollins, 1973) show that trees increase their yield under the influence of music. In response to the music played, some plants grew toward or away from the speakers. With certain music some plants even withered and died. Human beings are obviously also very sensitive to what they hear. John Beaulieu, naturopathic physician and music therapist, recalling his college days and the propensity of his friends for immersing themselves

yet popular language, often vivid and direct, speaks of head, heart, and guts in this connection. This is a rather simple and elementary, yet profound, observation. Such a framework provides a useful and practical model, grounded in a robust common sense and informed by keen psychological observation through centuries of practice. It can be developed into a very fine instrument for self observation as well as for gaining insight into others' behavior.

This was what Beaulieu was referring to. The music we hear is primarily apprehended by one center, emotional, intellectual, or active, although all music contains elements of each. Repeatedly acting on that center, it imparts its quality to our personality.

In military marches such as "The Battle Hymn of the Republic" we hear music inspiring strength and courage, therefore addressing itself to the active and emotional centers. Some rock and roll music that makes the pelvis gyrate hardly moves above the belt. Love and devotion, which obviously speak to the emotional center, are strongly evoked by the chants themselves. Baroque music—by Bach, Handel, or Vivaldi, for example—has a strong intellectual component and is related to the head, although the rhythm affects our active principle and the timbre and sonority, our emotions. Mozart's music seems to provide food for all three principles.

It may be interesting to note here that language, spoken or sung, is formed of consonantic and vocalic sounds. The consonants carry most of the information, the intelligence in a word, whereas the vowels carry the color and the emotional aspect of the meaning. Vowels are the result of the vibration produced by the flow of air on the vocal cords and in the speech organs. These sounds, in turn, resonate in the cavities of the body, in specific locations. Experimenting with the vowels U, O, A, E, and I, it is easy to verify that U resonates at the base of the spine; O, in the belly; A, in the chest or heart; E, in the throat; I, in the middle of the forehead, so that U and O are connected with the active principle, A, with the emotional, I, with the intellectual, and E participates in both intellectual and emotional. Thus these vowels have the power to tune these principles and the organs connected with them.

Consonants (meaning "sounding with") are simply used to start and stop the vocalic sounds. They limit and form the sounds, giving them intelligence. Latin is rich in vowels and this language therefore contributes to the emotional quality of Gregorian Chant. This is particularly apparent when vowels are sung over many notes, as in melismatic passages.

The resonance created in the bodies of the singers by the chanting of these vowels creates overtones high in frequency, which have an awakening effect. These are the charged sounds spoken of earlier.

It would be difficult to think of music that is more balanced than Gregorian Chant, rising and falling like the gentle ebb and flow of the sea. Neither attracting nor repelling, it remains centered at a point of rest and stability. It does not overwhelm us with sentiment but invites us to join in the devotion it calls forth. There is nothing in the music to set us thinking or incite us to action. Instead, it provides relief from the surfeit of ideas and activity that fatigues and weakens us, providing something that is of much greater importance: nourishment for the heart.

Internal Sound

◆

It would be a mistake if we thought of sound as only physical—what is perceivable by the ear. We also hear sound in our minds as echoes of what we have already heard, or as figments of our thoughts and imagination—subtle sounds perhaps, but nonetheless sounds. Tunes, voices, advertising jingles, and conversations circle like a merry-go-round. Throughout our days we are constantly listening to this din. These self-perpetuating thought patterns run on relatively unnoticed. We become especially aware of them when we try to fall asleep. We recognize the mechanically repetitious, catchy tune that simply will not stop insinuating its way into our head all day long, the often-rehearsed conversation that may never even take place.

All these sounds and music are playing within us continually, a kind of subtle and discordant orchestra never heard by anyone but ourselves. At times we hang on to this inner sonic baggage; at other times, we would just as soon send it off to a different destination and simply be quiet. The important thing to notice is that these sounds, for better or worse, act as a screen for whatever experience is coming our way. Like tinted sunglasses, they can completely change our perception of whatever is in front of us.

Every day we are in a position to choose, to a certain extent, what we place before our mind, what we give our attention to. As far as our selection of music is concerned, if we want the balanced, gracious, reasonable, and quite healthy approach to life, listening to Gregorian Chant is a good idea.

The Therapeutic Power of Chant

◆

In the same way that chanting mantra is said gradually to change the mind-set of the devotee, Gregorian Chant is designed to create awe, reverence, and gratitude in those who sing it and those who listen to it. It acts as a protection against the onslaught of less positive thoughts that take over the mind when it is not being watched. This positive effect of the chant is enhanced through the work of the liturgy in the monastic setting.

Gregorian Chant is fundamentally a communal and liturgical

activity that brings wholeness to communities. It was formulated when the state of society was at a low ebb and, as we have seen, it had a powerful influence in restoring a degree of cohesion and stability to the empire of Charlemagne. Gregorian Chant was not designed for curing individuals of any particular illness. However, if the individual is not well, then society cannot be well either. Gregorian Chant is prayer. As such, its effect depends on the grace of God and on the intentionality of the congregation: singers and listeners, healers and the healed, for they form a single community in the act of worship.

The effect of chant is to balance mind, emotions, and body. Singing or simply actively listening to chant with directed attention, we feel whole and part of a greater whole. It is precisely this integrating tendency that constitutes healing.

To heal is to make whole, but to heal is not necessarily to cure. The dying patient can be healed, though he cannot be cured. This was well understood in the early days of hospitals and hospices, when they were founded in the twelfth century. It is being rediscovered in our own day. Through chant, a dignity, awe, simplicity, directness, and detachment are brought into a situation culturally overlaid by denial and indifference.

The healing process begins with a desire for wholeness, a wholeness that is as encompassing as the state of consciousness of the community will allow. It demonstrates the degree of their attention, the strength of their faith, the perseverance of their effort. It is through the openness and generosity of their hearts that this radius of concern, shaped by tradition and limited only by the power of listening, expands from individuals to families, nations, humankind, and eventually to the sustained active communion with the whole creation of a Francis of Assisi. Here in his words we find the culmination of this power of love, cultivated by the chant, resonating with clarity and balance on a global scale, bringing peace and healing even among the elements:

Be thou praised, my Lord, of Sister Water which is much useful and humble and precious and pure. Be thou praised, my Lord, of Brother Fire, by which Thou has lightened the night. And he is beautiful and joyful and robust and strong. Be thou praised, my Lord, of our sister Mother Earth which sustains us and hath us in rule, And produces diverse fruits with colored flowers and herbs.

The surge of interest in chant may perhaps be telling us that the time has come to address our problems differently, forgetting old, tired paradigms of failed wars, be they wars on poverty or on crime. Perhaps a belief is at large that there is still enough power in the ancient chants to tame the wolves stalking our cities with their Uzis as Francis tamed the wolf at Gubbio, or to care for the homeless who are clearly becoming a new class, a new order, in society beside the managerial class and the dwindling class of the fully employed. The have-nots, the have-it-alls, and the have-it-as-the-have-it-alls-decide undoubtedly constitute a new feudal order for the new millennium.

If the present interest in Gregorian Chant is indicative of future trends, perhaps with enough persistence this new generation will have as much luck with its songs in building a new order, as the passing one had in bringing down walls, curtains, and screens of brick, iron, and smoke.

CHAPTER 8

THE LIFE OF CHANT

In this book we have explained Gregorian Chant in the context of its philosophical and religious setting and traced its history through the Middle Ages. We have spoken of chant as a devotional music holding sacred words of scripture and used in the Mass and the Divine Office. Briefly explaining its construction and the way it is sung, we have then emphasized the value of giving chant our full attention when we listen to it.

We live in a society in which people are often pushed past their endurance, in which there is constant demand on all their resources. The requirements of a job, the care of elderly parents, the education of children, and civil and even religious responsibilities assail us on all sides. We are frequently in a situation where there is no rest and little refreshment. The tasks multiply and we feel that there is no time, even to breathe.

"Music to the rescue," we say to ourselves and turn it on. Unfortunately much of what is available will simply not be helpful in our situation. Even if the music is romantic, classical, or "new age," it may serve only to increase our sense of agitation. Pieces intended to provide space for relaxation are often simply "spacey" and add to the sense of confusion and lack of focus that we are already experiencing.

What is needed is music that will help us to relax without becoming too lax. It is here that chant can truly help. If we are willing to give it our full attention, the sound of its ancient melodies will draw us into a quiet, yet lively place where we will find the refreshment that we so desperately seek.

As we broaden our sphere of awareness through listening to consciously uttered sounds, our own sphere of being—what we experience as our space—opens up. The rush of events seems to slow down. By the clock nothing has changed, yet we have a different perception of the things that are happening. Suddenly time is given back to us; we have enough and more to spare. In order to come into this state of alertness and receptivity a little effort is necessary: a willingness to listen, and a spirit of active, rather than passive, participation.

Whether or not one is a true believer—and those who say that they are, all the time and in all circumstances, are few and far between—is not of primary importance. In the same way that we do not need to subscribe fully to the tenets of Hinduism in order to enter fully into the spirit and intention of yoga and benefit from its healthful effect on mind and body, so it is with our participation in the life of chant. It is not necessary to be a believing Christian to be a part of this music, but rather it is a matter of suspending disbelief. As when going to the opera or a play we have to be willing to "enter the myth" and go along with it in order to partake of an experience grounded in our common humanity.

Chant calls us first and foremost to a sense of unity, a unity that exists between singer, listener, and the sound itself. It invites us to join together for a few moments in what is essentially an act of worship. We fall still, and then quietly and gently the chant rises. We are carried along together on the crest of its wave—men and women celebrating our humanity and our divinity. As the wave touches back to shore we remain awake and more at rest. We have experienced what Jacques Maritain speaks of as "the intercommunion of all things, among themselves and with us, in the creative flow from which all existence comes."

In closing, let us listen to what may be considered two of the most beautiful examples of Western music ever composed. They are selections sung by the monks of Santo Domingo de Silos on tracks 3 and 7 of *Chant*, but they are also found on many other recordings. You will see that if you are listening to the music at the same time, it will be easy to follow the rise and fall of the melody as noted by neumes in traditional notation.

Christus factus est pro nobis, the text of which is taken from the New Testament Epistle of Paul to the Philippians (Chapter 2, verses 8–9), is the Gradual or response to the epistle read for the Mass on Thursday of Holy Week.

Hrí-stus fáctus est pro nó- bis obé - di - ens us- que ad mór-tem, mór-tem au-tem crú-cis. ℣ Propter quod et Dé-us exaltávit íllum, et dé- dit íl-li nó- men, quod est super ómne nó- men.

Christ became obedient for us unto death, even to death on the cross. Therefore God has exalted him and has bestowed on him a name that is above all names.

The opening portion of the text—"Christ became obedient for us unto death"—is sung all through the day on Holy Thursday (the day before Christ's Crucifixion, when, in the presence of his disciples, he spoke of his impending death and his acceptance of it) at the end of each of the Hours. This practice is continued on Good Friday (the day of the Crucifixion), except that the next portion, "even to death on the cross," is added. On Holy Saturday, when the whole church stands in silence and awe, awaiting the day of Resurrection, the entire text is sung, adding the words, "Therefore God has exalted him and has bestowed on him a name that is above all names."

The song of praise begins in a low and solemn way, then emphasizes that Christ's sacrifice was accepted by him as required by God (*obediens*) and was complete, even to death on a cross. All this is stated in a single, long, balanced wave of sounds. Then, after hesitating on the word *autem*, "even," as if afraid to speak out, the music descends radically to admit that the death was shameful and upon a cross. The chant then hastens to add, on a rising wave of triumph, that it was exactly for this reason (*propter quod*) that God raised him up (*exaltavit illum*) higher than the tree on which he was hung, giving him a name—and here the song falls in awe to intone *quod est super omne nomen,* "which is above all other names," and belongs to God, the unnameable.

It is appropriate to conclude with a beginning. Here the musical example is an Introit, or entrance song, for the Mass of Pentecost. The text is taken from the Old Testament apocryphal book of Wisdom of Solomon, Chapter I, verse 7. It is track 7 on the *Chant* disk.

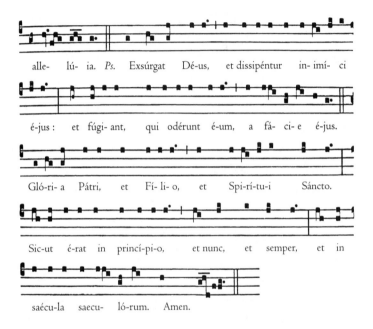

alle- lú- ia. *Ps.* Exsúrgat Dé-us, et dissipéntur in-imí- ci

é-jus: et fúgi-ant, qui odérunt é-um, a fá-ci-e é-jus.

Gló-ri-a Pátri, et Fí-li-o, et Spi-rí-tu-i Sáncto.

Sic-ut é-rat in princí-pi-o, et nunc, et semper, et in

saécu-la saecu- ló-rum. Amen.

The Spirit of the Lord fills the whole orb of earth, alleluia, and that which contains all things has knowledge of the voice, alleluia, alleluia, alleluia. ℣. Let God arise, and his enemies be scattered; let those who hate him flee from before his face.

℣. Glory to the Father, and to the Son, and to the Holy Spirit: as it was in the beginning, is now, and ever shall be through all ages. Amen. The Spirit of the Lord . . .

In the context of the Mass, the Introit always states the deepest meaning of the feast being celebrated. Here the music rises on *Spiritus Domini replevit orbem terrarum*, "The Spirit of the Lord fills the whole orb of earth," soaring upward on the word *replevit* (fills) to demonstrate the extent of the filling. The notes remain still and poised as the orb of earth (*orbem terrarum*) stands in awe, ready to receive. The joyous response, *Alleluia,* (praise to Yahweh) completes the musical clause.

Filled with a profound sense of mystery, the text continues, "and that which contains all things has knowledge of the voice." The music is demonstrative at *quod* (that), and expressively rounded at *omnia* (all things), preparatory to proclaiming the Spirit's full knowledge of the voice (*scientiam habet vocis*). A triple *Alleluia* is then sung with a joy that is both relieved and accepting.

Using an ancient melodic formula, cantors then sing the first verse of Psalm 68: "Let God arise, and his enemies be scattered;

let those who hate him flee from before his face." This is followed by a doxology, or liturgical formula of praise, to the Trinity of Father, Son, and Holy Spirit, and there is a return to the initial antiphon, *"Spiritus Domini."*

The Feast of Pentecost, celebrated here, brings us to the moment of sharing whatever has been realized, bringing it to its fullest expression. The vision of creation expressed by this chant, and by chant in general, is one in which the life of humanity is ever more surely becoming the Divine Life. Its sound is unified, loving, and merciful, pointing to healing and wholeness.

Each time we listen to the singing of the monks, we are invited to share in the music, not as outsiders who, from a different time, place, or tradition, listen with interest to these ancient songs but remain apart from them. Rather, we should listen as companions, joining to the song of the monks all of our own experiences, our own songs of praise and thanksgiving, coming from the heart.

Many fine recordings of Gregorian Chant are no longer available, but now that it has become so popular, many more are being released. The following are some of those available at the time of publication:

Chant: The Benedictine Monks of Santo Domingo de Silos. Angel Records CDC: 55138.

Chant Noel: The Benedictine Monks of Santo Domingo de Silos. Angel Records CDC: 55193.

Chant 101: An Introduction to Chant. Charlotte A. Miller. Cassette. Examples of Sanskrit and Gregorian Chant. Not in many stores but available from Enlightenment, P.O. Box 87528, Phoenix, Ariz. 85080-7528. 602-789-1105.

Easter. Monastic Choir of St. Peter's Abbey, Solesmes, directed by Dom Jean Claire. Paraclete. CD: S822.

Gregorian Chant. Benedictine Monks of the Abbey of St. Maurice & St. Maur, Clervaux. Philips Classical. CD: 432 506.

Gregorian Chant: The Choir of Carmelite Priory, London. John McCarthy. London Jubilee/Decca. CD: 425 729.

Gregorian Chant: Choralschola of the Niederaltaicher Scholaren. Konrad Ruhland, conductor. Sony Classical. CD: SK53899.

Gregorian Chant: The Ecclesiastical Year in Gregorian Chant. Schola Cantorum of Amsterdam Students. Sony Essential Classics. CD: SBK 47670.

Gregorian Chant by the Benedictine Sisters. Ave Maria Vol. II. Invincible. CD: INVCD I.

Gregorian Chants for All Seasons. Choir of the Vienna Hofburgkapelle. Josef Schabasser. Vox Box. 2 CDs or 3 cassettes: 5010.

Immortel Grégorien. Voyages dans l'Année Grégorienne. Various monastic choirs. Studio SM. Vols. I and II. CDs: 12 15 82 and 12 15 84.

The Tradition of Gregorian Chant. Various monastic choirs. Archiv CD: 435 032.

Track 1: *Puer natus est nobis*

Puer natus est nobis, et filius datus est nobis: cuius imperium super humerum eius, et vocabitur nomen eius magni consilii angelus.

℣. Cantate domino canticum novum, quia mirabilia fecit. ℣. Gloria patri, et filio, et spiritui sancto: sicut erat in principio, et nunc et semper, et in sæcula sæculorum. Amen. Puer natus est nobis . . .

Track 2: *Os iusti*

Os iusti meditabitur sapientiam, et lingua eius loquetur iudicium.

℣. Lex dei eius in corde ipsius, et non supplantabuntur gressus eius.

Track 3: *Christus factus est pro nobis (see page 147 for music)*

Christus factus est pro nobis obediens usque ad mortem, mortem autem crucis.

℣. Propter quod et deus exaltavit illum, et dedit illi nomen, quod est super omne nomen.

Track 4: *Mandatum novum do vobis*

Mandatum novum do vobis: ut diligatis invicem, sicut dilexi vos, dicit dominus.
Ecce quam bonum et quam iucundum, habitare fratres in unum!
Sicut unguentum in capite, quod descendit in barbam, barbam aaron:
Quod descendit in oram vestimenti eius, sicut ros hermon, qui descendit in montem sion:
Quoniam illic mandavit dominus benedictionem, et vitam usque in sæculum.
Mandatum novum . . .

Track 5: *Media vita in morte sumus*

Media vita in morte sumus: quem quærimus adiutorem, nisi te domine?
qui pro peccatis nostris iuste irasceris. *Sancte deus, sancte fortis, sancte misericors salvator, amaræ morti ne tradas nos.

Track 1: *The Introit for the Third Mass of Christmas*
A child is born to us, a son is given to us: his shoulders shall bear princely power, and his name shall be called Angel of Great Counsel.
℣. Sing the Lord a new song, for wonders have been done. ℣. Glory to the Father, and to the Son, and to the Holy Spirit: as it was in the beginning, is now, and ever shall be through all ages. Amen. A child is born to us . . .

Track 2: *The Gradual of the Mass for Doctors of the Church*
The mouth of the just one shall meditate wisdom, and his tongue shall speak judgment. ℣. The law of God is in his heart, and his steps shall not falter.

Track 3: *The Gradual for the Mass of Thursday in Holy Week (see page 147 for music)*
Christ became obedient for us unto death, even to death on the cross.
℣. Therefore God has exalted him and has bestowed on him a name that is above all names.

Track 4: *Antiphon & Psalm sung during the Washing of Feet on Thursday in Holy Week*
A new commandment I give you: that you love one another, as I have loved you.
See, how good and pleasant it is for brothers to dwell together in unity!
Like precious oil on the head that ran down the beard, the beard of Aaron,
that ran down to the hem of his garment—like the dew of Hermon, that falls on Mount Sion:
For there the Lord has commanded blessing, life throughout the ages.
A new commandment . . .

Track 5: *Processional Responsory for the Sundays immediately preceding Lent*
In the midst of life, we are in death: from whom should we seek help, if not you, Lord? Though for our sins you would justly be angry. *Holy God, holy strong one, holy and merciful savior, do not betray us to bitter death.

℣. In te speraverunt patres nostri; speraverunt, et liberasti eos. *Sancte deus . . .

℣. Ad te clamaverunt patres nostri; clamaverunt, et non sunt confusi. *Sancte deus . . .

℣. Gloria patri, et filio, et spiritui sancto. *Sancte deus . . .

Track 6: *Alleluia/Beatus vir qui suffert*
Alleluia, alleluia. ℣. Beatus vir, qui suffert tentationem: quoniam cum probatus fuerit, accipiet coronam vitæ. Alleluia.

Track 7: *Spiritus domini (see page 149 for music)*
Spiritus domini replevit orbem terrarum, alleluia: et hoc quod continet omnia, scientiam habet vocis, alleluia, alleluia, alleluia.

℣. Exsurgat deus, et dissipentur inimici eius: et fugiant, qui oderunt eum, a facie eius. ℣. Gloria patri, et filio, et spiritui sancto: sicut erat in principio, et nunc et semper, et in sæcula sæculorum. Amen. Spiritus domini . . .

Track 8: *Improperium*
Improperium exspectavit cor meum, et miseriam: et sustinui qui simul mecum contristaretur, et non fuit: consolantem me quæsivi, et non inveni: et dederunt in escam meam fel, et in siti mea potaverunt me aceto.

Track 9: *Lætatus sum*
Lætatus sum in his quæ dicta sunt mihi: in domum domini ibimus.

℣. Fiat pax in virtute tua, et abundantia in turribus tuis.

Track 10: *Kyrie (each petition is sung twice)*
Kyrie eleison. Christe eleison. Kyrie eleison.

Track 11: *Puer natus in Bethlehem*
Puer natus in Bethlehem, alleluia: unde gaudet ierusalem, alleluia, alleluia.

℣. In you our fathers hoped: they hoped, and you freed them. *Holy God . . .

℣. To you our fathers cried: they cried, and they were not disappointed.
*Holy God . . .

℣. Glory to the Father, and to the Son, and to the Holy Spirit. *Holy God . . .

Track 6: *Alleluia for the Mass that is common to Confessors*
Alleluia, alleluia. ℣. Blessed is the one who endures temptation: when he has been proven, he shall receive the crown of life. Alleluia.

Track 7: *The Introit for the Mass of Pentecost (see page 149 for music)*
The Spirit of the Lord fills the whole orb of earth, alleluia, and that which contains all things has knowledge of the voice, alleluia, alleluia, alleluia.

℣. Let God arise, and his enemies be scattered; let those who hate him flee from before his face. ℣. Glory to the Father, and to the Son, and to the Holy Spirit: as it was in the beginning, is now and ever shall be through all ages. Amen. The Spirit of the Lord . . .

Track 8: *The Offertory for the Mass on Palm Sunday*
My heart expected reproach and misery: I looked for someone to grieve with me, but there was none, and to comfort me, and found no one: but they fed my hunger with gall, and in my thirst they gave me vinegar to drink.

Track 9: *The Gradual for the Fourth Sunday in Lent*
I rejoiced when they said to me: We will go unto the house of the Lord.
℣. Peace shall be in your strength, and abundance in your towers.

Track 10: *A part of the Ordinary of the Mass (each petition is sung twice)*
Lord, have mercy. Christ, have mercy. Lord, have mercy.

Track 11: *A 14th-century metrical Christmas Hymn*
A child is born in Bethlehem, alleluia: Jerusalem rejoices, alleluia, alleluia.

*In cordis iubilo christum natum adoremus, cum novo cantico.
Assumpsit carnem filius, alleluia, dei patris altissimus . . . *In cordis . . .
In hoc natali gaudio, alleluia, BENEDICAMUS DOMINO . . . *In cordis . . .
Laudetur sancta trinitas, alleluia, DEO dicamus GRATIAS . . . *In cordis . . .

Track 12: *Jacta cogitatum tuum*

Jacta cogitatum tuum in domino, et ipse te enutriet. ℣. Dum clamarem ad dominum, exaudivit vocem meam ab his, qui appropinquant mihi. Jacta . . .

Track 13: *Verbum caro factum est*

Verbum caro factum est, et habitavit in nobis: *et vidimus gloriam eius, gloriam quasi unigeniti a patre, plenum gratiæ et veritatis.

℣. In principio erat verbum, et v erbum erat apud deum, et deus erat verbum.
*et vidimus . . .

℣. Gloria patri, et filio, et spiritui sancto; *et vidimus . . .

Track 14: *Genuit puerpera regem*

Genuit puerpera regem, cui nomen æternum, et gaudia matris habens cum virginitatis honore: nec primam similem visa est, nec habere sequentem, alleluia.
Jubilate deo omnis terra, servite domino in lætitia.
Introite in conspectu eius, in exsultatione.
Scitote quoniam dominus ipse est deus: ipse fecit nos, et non ipsi nos.
Populus eius, et oves pascuæ eius: introite portas eius in confessione, atria eius in hymnis, confitemini illi.
Laudate nomen eius: quoniam suavis est dominus, in æternum misericordia eius, et usque in generationem et generationem veritas eius.
Genuit puerpera regem . . .

*With sounds of rejoicing, let us praise Christ's birth in a new song.

The son of the highest Father, alleluia, assumes human flesh . . . *With sounds . . .

In this joyous night, alleluia, LET US BLESS THE LORD . . . *With sounds . . .

In praise of the holy Trinity, alleluia: THANKS BE TO GOD . . . *With sounds . . .

Track 12: *The Gradual of the Mass for the first Thursday in Lent*

Cast your cares upon the Lord, and the Lord will sustain you. ℣. When I called upon the Lord, the Lord heard my voice and rescued me from my enemies.

Cast your cares . . .

Track 13: *A Responsory for the Office of Matins on Christmas*

The Word was made flesh, and dwelt among us: *and we saw his glory, the glory of the only begotten of the Father, full of grace and truth.

℣. In the beginning was the Word, and the Word was with God, and the Word was God; *and we saw . . .

℣. Glory to the Father, and to the Son, and to the Holy Spirit; *and we saw . . .

Track 14: *Antiphon with Psalm from the Office of Lauds on Christmas*

Having given birth to the king whose name is eternal, the young mother's joy is mixed with a virgin's honor: there was never one like her before, nor shall there ever be, alleluia.

Sing joyfully to God, all the earth, serve the Lord with gladness.

Enter his presence with exceeding great joy. Know that the Lord is God: he made us, and not we ourselves.

We are his people and the sheep of his pasture: enter his gates with praise, go into his courts with hymns and give him glory.

Praise his name: for the Lord is sweet, his mercy endures for ever, and his truth from generation to generation.

Having given birth to the king . . .

Track 15: *Oculi omnium*

Oculi omnium in te sperant, domine: et tu das illis escam in tempore opportuno.

℣. Aperis tu manum tuam: et imples omne animal benedictione.

Track 16: *Ave mundi spes maria*

Ave mundi spes maria, ave mitis, ave pia, ave plena gratia.
Ave virgo singularis, quæ per rubum designaris non passum incendia.
Ave rosa speciosa, ave iesse virgula:
Cuius fructus nostri luctus relaxavit vincula.
Ave cuius viscera contra mortis fœdera ediderunt filium.
Ave carens simili, mundo diu flebili reparasti gaudium.
Ave virginum lucerna, per quam fulsit lux superna his quos umbra tenuit.
Ave virgo de qua nasci, et de cuius lacte pasci rex cælorum voluit.
Ave gemma cœli luminarium.
Ave sancti spiritus sacrarium.
O quam mirabilis, et quam laudabilis hæc est virginitas!
In qua per spiritum facta paraclitum fulsit fœcunditas.
O quam sancta, quam serena, quam benigna, quam amœna esse virgo creditur!
Per quam servitus finitur, porta cœli aperitur, et libertas redditur.
O castitatis lilium, tuum precare filium, qui salus est humilium:
Ne nos pro nostro vitio, in flebili iudicio subjiciat supplicio.
Sed nos tua sancta prece mundans a peccati fæce collocet in lucis domo.
Amen dicat omnis homo.

Track 17: *Kyrie, fons bonitatis*

Kyrie, fons bonitatis, pater ingenite, a quo bona cuncta procedunt, eleison.
Kyrie, qui pati natum mundi pro crimine, ipsum ut salvaret misisti, eleison.
Kyrie, qui septiformis dans dona pneumatis, a quo cœlum, terra replentur, eleison.

Track 15: *The Gradual of the Mass for the fourth Thursday in Lent*
The eyes of all hope in you, Lord, and you grant them nourishment in due season.
℣. You open your hand, and all creatures are filled with blessing.

Track 16: *A mid-15th-century Sequence honoring Mary*
Hail the world's hope, Mary, hail the mild, hail the holy, hail full of grace.
Hail singular virgin, signified by the burning bush that was not consumed.
Hail beautiful rose, hail shoot of Jesse,
Whose mourning fruit loosened our chains.
Hail, whose womb brought forth a son in a covenant against death.
Hail, without equal, who restored joy to a wretched world.
Hail lamp of virginity, whose light shone on those whom shadows held.
Hail virgin, ordained to bear, suckle, and nourish the king of heaven.
Hail heavenly jewel of lights.
Hail shrine of the Holy Spirit.
O how wonderful and praiseworthy is this virginity!
In it the Comforter shone fruitfulness in the spirit.
O how holy, how serene, how gentle, how pleasant to belong to this virgin!
Through whom servitude is ended, heaven's door opened, and liberty restored.
O chaste lily, entreat your son, the savior of the humble:
Let not our corruption subject us to wretched judgment, we pray,
But let your holy prayer cleanse our sins and draw us to the home of light.
Let all humankind sing Amen.

Track 17: *A part of the Ordinary of the Mass (with the original text troped or expanded)*
Lord, fount of goodness, unbegotten father and source of all good, have mercy.
Lord, born to cleanse the world of sin, sent to save us, have mercy.
Lord, giver of sevenfold gifts, by whom heaven fills the earth, have mercy.

Christe, unice dei patris genite, quem de virgine nasciturum mundo mirifice, sancti prœdixerunt prophetæ, eleison.

Christe, hagie cœli compos regiæ, melos glorie cui semper adstans pro numine angelorum decantat apex, eleison.

Christe, cœlitus adsis nostris precibus, pronis mentibus quem in terris devote colimus, ad te pie iesu clamantes, eleison.

Kyrie, spiritus alme, cohœrens patri natoque unius usiæ consistendo, flans ab utroque, eleison.

Kyrie, qui baptizato in iordanis unda christo, effulgens specie columbina apparuisti, eleison.

Kyrie, ignis divine, pectora nostra succende, ut digni pariter proclamare possimus semper, eleison.

Track 18: *Veni, sancte spiritus*

Veni, sancte spiritus, et emitte cœlitus lucis tuæ radium.

Veni, pater pauperum, veni, datur munerum, veni, lumen cordium.

Consolator optime, dulcis hospes animæ, dulce refrigerium.

In labore requies, in æstu temperies, in fletu solatium.

O lux beatissima, reple cordis intima tuorum fidelium.

Sine tuo numine, nihil est in homine, nihil est innoxium.

Lava quod est sordidum, riga quod est aridum, sana quod est saucium,

Flecte quod est rigidum, fove quod est frigidum, rege quod est devium.

Da tuis fidelibus, in te confidentibus, sacrum septenarium.

Da virtutis meritum, da salutis exitum, da perenne gaudium.

Track 19: *Hosanna filio david*

Hosanna filio david: benedictus qui venit in nomine domini.

Rex israel: Hosanna in excelsis!

Christ, only begotten son of God the Father, wondrously born of a virgin into the world as the prophets foretold, have mercy.

Christ, who stirs with heavenly power the melody of glory, who stands before the strength of singing angels, have mercy.

Christ, whom we on earth faithfully worship with humble minds, from heaven hear our prayer as we cry to you, Jesus: have mercy.

Lord, kind Spirit joined to Father and Son, living with and flowing from both, have mercy.

Lord, splendrous in the form of a dove when Christ was baptized in the Jordan, have mercy.

Lord, ignite our hearts with divine fire, so we may always cry out worthily: have mercy.

Track 18: *The Sequence of the Mass for Pentecost*
Come, Holy Spirit, and give from heaven the light of your radiance.
Come, Father of the poor, come, giver of gifts, come, light for hearts.
Best of consolers, the soul's delightful guest, sweet refreshment.
Rest from our labors, coolness in the heat, solace in our woes.
O most blessed light, fill the deepest hearts of your faithful.
Without your light, humankind has naught, nothing is innocent.
Wash what is soiled, strengthen what is dry, heal what is wounded.
Bend what is stiff, melt what is frozen, straighten the devious.
Grant to your faithful, who trust in you, your sevenfold gifts.
Grant virtue to our service, grant health to our going-forth, grant us eternal joy.

Track 19: *Antiphon sung during the Blessing of Palms on Palm Sunday in Holy Week*
Hosanna to the Son of David: blessed is he who comes in the name of the Lord.
King of Israel: Hosanna in the highest.

In the preparation of this book, I have referred frequently to five works by eminent scholars in the area of chant and medieval music:

Gregorian Chant by Willi Apel (Bloomington: Indiana University Press, 1958)

"Rhythm in Western Sacred Music before the Mid-Twelfth Century" by R. John Blackley, to be published by Schola Antiqua in 1995

"Rhythmic Interpretation of Chant" by R. John Blackley, in *The Hymnal 1982 Companion*, ed. Raymond Glover (New York: Church Hymnal Corporation, 1990)

Western Plainchant: A Handbook by David Hiley (Oxford: Clarendon Press, 1993)

Medieval Music by Richard H. Hoppins (New York: W. W. Norton & Co., 1978)

Without these valuable resources, my work would have been impossible.

Two books have provided me with sensitive insight into medieval monastic life: *The Journal of Hildegard of Bingen* by Barbara Lachman (New York: Bell Tower, 1993) and Esther de Waal's *Seeking God: The Way of St. Benedict* (Collegeville, Minnesota: The Liturgical Press, 1984).

I thank Don Campbell, director of the Institute for Music, Health and Education in Boulder, Colorado and author or editor of numerous books on the effect of sound and healing, for knowledge of the emerging field of sound therapy, coming, in particular, from his two anthologies—*Music Physician for Times to Come* (1991) and its companion, *Music and Miracles* (1992)—and the short volume *The Roar of Silence: Healing Powers of Breath, Tone and Music* (1989). All three are published in Wheaton, Illinois by the Theosophical Publishing House.

I have listened with great interest to Mr. Campbell's audio tapes: *Healing with Tone and Chant* (also from the Theosophical Publishing House) and *Healing with Great*

Music (from Sounds True Recordings in Boulder, Colorado) and to the interview conducted by Tim Wilson with French physician Dr. Alfred Tomatis, recorded on audiotape, *The Healing Power of Voice and Ear,* available through the Institute for Music, Health and Education in Boulder, Colorado. Further information about Dr. Tomatis may also be found in his autobiography *The Conscious Ear: My Life of Transformation Through Listening* (Barrytown, New York: Station Hill Press, 1991).

I wish to acknowledge, as well, a conversation with John Beaulieu that whetted my interest in sound and healing and Dr. Beaulieu's useful book *Music and Sound in the Healing Arts* (Barrytown, New York: Station Hill Press, 1991). Further insights on the ways that music affects us physically, mentally, and emotionally are presented in Randall McClellan's fascinating volume, *The Healing Forces of Music: Healing, Theory and Practice* (Amity, New York: Amity House, 1988).

For those wishing guidance in choosing music helpful in a variety of life situations, I would suggest Hal A. Lingerman's *The Healing Energies of Music* (Wheaton, Illinois: Theosophical Publishing House, 1983). Hans Jenny's beautiful pictorial volume entitled *Cymatics* (Basle, Switzerland: Basilius Presse, Volume I, 1967; Volume II, 1972) vividly illustrates the effect of sound vibration in material substances.

Recently I was overjoyed to be invited to attend a rehearsal of the Schola Antiqua in Baltimore, Maryland. During an entire evening I received the restorative and enriching benefits of chant. For this I am deeply grateful to Schola members Meredith Brown, Auguste Fortin, Savitri Gauthier, Jenna Isennock, and director R. John Blackley, all of whom inspired me in my work by the harmonious blending of their voices and the devotion with which they sang.

Thanks, also, to David Smith for his beautiful singing for us of the early church music.

I would like to express gratitude to my sisters and brothers from Chrysalis House (Contemplative Outreach) in Warwick, New York for showing me how all of life can become prayer, and to the staff of St. Paul's Church, Englewood, New Jersey, who demonstrate how the liturgy translates itself into attentive and caring service.

To my loving and dependable friend, Toinette Lippe, I owe not only the initial inspiration for this endeavor but its nurturing in every respect. I appreciate her careful editing, even more her ability to see so clearly what is needed and provide assistance without delay.

My husband, Jean Le Mée, has closely followed the development of the book, offering me the benefits of his scholarship and deep understanding of the wisdom of the Middle Ages. His clarity and devotion have lighted my life for more than thirty years.

I thank my fun-loving daughter Hannah for her cheerful support and for reminding me that we don't have to listen to Gregorian Chant *all* the time.

Finally, I wish to remember with deep appreciation my dear aunt Kie who, through her utter devotion to the three Bs—Bach, Beethoven, and Brahms—first initiated me into the joy of music.

Katharine Le Mée

Katharine Le Mée has a Ph.D. in Romance Linguistics from Columbia University and has taught French for many years in colleges and high schools. Both as a singer and conductor, she has immersed herself in the monophonic and polyphonic music of the Middle Ages. She and her husband, Dr. Jean Le Mée, have frequently given workshops on the music and the sacred art and architecture of twelfth-century France. Dr. Le Mée lives in Englewood, New Jersey, with her husband and her daughter, Hannah.

OTHER BELL TOWER BOOKS

Books that nourish the soul, illuminate the mind, and speak directly to the heart

Valeria Alfeyeva. PILGRIMAGE TO DZHVARI: *A Woman's Journey of Spiritual Awakening.* 0-517-59194-4 Hardcover

David A. Cooper. ENTERING THE SACRED MOUNTAIN: *A Mystical Odyssey.* 0-517-59653-9 Hardcover

————. THE HEART OF STILLNESS: *The Elements of Spiritual Practice.* 0-517-58621-5 Hardcover; 0-517-88187-X Softcover

————. SILENCE, SIMPLICITY, AND SOLITUDE: *A Guide for Spiritual Retreat.* 0-517-88186-1 Softcover

James G. Cowan. LETTERS FROM A WILD STATE: *Rediscovering Our True Relationship to Nature.* 0-517-58770-X Hardcover

————. MESSENGERS OF THE GODS: *Tribal Elders Reveal the Ancient Wisdom of the Earth.* 0-517-88078-4 Softcover

Marc David. NOURISHING WISDOM: *A Mind/Body Approach to Nutrition and Well-Being.* 0-517-57636-8 Hardcover; 0-517-88129-2 Softcover

Kat Duff. THE ALCHEMY OF ILLNESS. 0-517-88097-0 Softcover

Noela N. Evans. MEDITATIONS FOR THE PASSAGES AND CELEBRATIONS OF LIFE: *A Book of Vigils.* 0-517-59341-6 Hardcover; 0-517-88299-X Softcover

Burghild Nina Holzer. A WALK BETWEEN HEAVEN AND EARTH: *A Personal Journal on Writing and the Creative Process.* 0-517-88096-2 Softcover

Greg Johanson and Ron Kurtz GRACE UNFOLDING: *Psychotherapy in the Spirit of the Tao-te ching.* 0-517-88130-6 Softcover

Selected by Marcia and Jack Kelly. ONE HUNDRED GRACES: *Mealtime Blessings.* 0-517-58567-7 Hardcover; 0-517-88230-2 Softcover

Jack and Marcia Kelly. SANCTUARIES: *A Guide to Lodgings in Monasteries, Abbeys, and Retreats of the United States.* THE NORTHEAST 0-517-57727-5 Softcover; WEST COAST & SOUTHWEST. 0-517-88007-5 Softcover

Barbara Lachman. THE JOURNAL OF HILDEGARD OF BINGEN. 0-517-59169-3 Hardcover

Gunilla Norris. BECOMING BREAD: *Meditations on Loving and Transformation.* 0-517-59168-5 Hardcover

BEING HOME: *A Book of Meditations.* 0-517-58159-0 Hardcover

————. JOURNEYING IN PLACE: *Reflections from a Country Garden.* 0-517-59762-4 Hardcover

————. SHARING SILENCE: *Meditation Practice and Mindful Living.* 0-517-59506-0 Hardcover

Ram Dass and Mirabai Bush. COMPASSION IN ACTION: *Setting Out on the Path of Service.* 0-517-57635-X Softcover

Richard Whelan, ed.. SELF-RELIANCE: *The Wisdom of Ralph Waldo Emerson as Inspiration for Daily Living.* 0-517-58512-X Softcover

Bell Tower books are for sale at your local bookstore or you may call Random House at 1-800-793-BOOK to order with a credit card.

Sitivit anima mea ad deum vivum quando veniã z apparebo ante faciem domini. Quemadmodum. Memoria eterna erit iusti. Ab auditione. m. non timebit. etc.